Highlights of
COLLEGE
FOOTBALL

by
John Durant and Les Etter

HASTINGS HOUSE, PUBLISHERS

NEW YORK

796.33

Published simultaneously in Canada by
Saunders, of Toronto, Ltd., Don Mills, Ontario

ISBN: 8038-3013-0

Library of Congress Catalog Card Number: 76-130045
Printed in the United States of America

304176

Contents

CHAPTER 1
Ancient Football Around the World   1

CHAPTER 2
The Game Comes to America   11

CHAPTER 3
The Eastern Colleges Make the First Rules   24

CHAPTER 4
Walter Camp, the Father of American Football   35

CHAPTER 5
Heroes of the Early Gridiron   51

CHAPTER 6
The Game Sweeps the Country and Comes of Age   74

CHAPTER 7
The Golden Age and the Glamor Boys   110

CHAPTER 8
Passes, Power and Depression   128

CHAPTER 9
The New T and the Touchdown Twins   147

CHAPTER 10
The Rise and Fall of the Platoons — The Fifties   162

CHAPTER 11
The Scoring System Changes   175

CHAPTER 12
The Platoons Return — More Touchdowns   184

CHAPTER 13
College Football — an American Heritage   203

APPENDIX
The Teams and Their Nicknames   205
The All-Time All-American Teams   207
Awards and Trophies   208
Longest Winning Streaks   209
The Bowl Games — Major Results
    Rose Bowl, Orange Bowl, Cotton Bowl, Sugar Bowl   211

INDEX   213

CHAPTER 1

Ancient Football
Around the World

No one can say with any certainty where or when football was first played, but it is known that the game goes back to antiquity and has been popular under various rules in many different parts of the world.

Long before the Christian era the Greeks were kicking a football up and down a field that had side lines, a center line, and goal lines. The ancient Romans played the game, and so did the Chinese (from 300 B.C. to about 500 A.D.) At the same time many savage tribes, lacking any contact with civilization or with one another, were playing their own brand of football. Among these primitive people were the Maoris of New Zealand, the Polynesians of the South Pacific, the Greenland Eskimos and the Celts of prehistoric Ireland. In other words, they were kicking the stuffing out of a football 2,000 years ago.

Throughout history wherever football was played, the basic idea of the game was the same — to move the ball forward to the opponent's goal — and this is so today. The resemblance of some of the ancient forms of football to the modern sport is striking. For example, in the old Greek game, which was called *Harpaston,* the

1

Eskimos playing football in Greenland, ca. 1725.

opposing teams met on a rectangular field and the players tried to advance the ball by kicking it, passing it or carrying it across the opposite goal line. Here were the elements of modern games such as soccer, Rugby, American football, and others.

In Greenland thousands of miles from the *Harpaston* fields, stone-age men who had never heard of Greece were playing a similar game. This was the Eskimo version of football.

The first white man to describe it was Hans Egede, a Norwegian missionary, who arrived in Greenland in 1721 and stayed 15 years.

In his book, *A Description of Greenland*, Egede wrote of the Eskimos:

"Ball playing is their most common diversion, which they play two different ways. They divide themselves into two parties; the first party players throw the ball to each other while those of the second party endeavor to get it from them.

"The second manner is like our playing at Foot-ball. They mark out two Barriers, at 3 or 4 hundred Paces distance one from the other; then being divided into two parties as before, they meet at the Starting Place, which is at the Midway between the two Barriers, and the Ball being thrown upon the ground, they strive who first shall get at it, and kick it with the Foot, each party towards their Barrier. He that is the most nimble-footed and dextrous at it, kicking the Ball before him, and gets the first to the Barrier, has won the Match."

This game, which the Eskimos developed by themselves, was not too different from soccer as it is played today. Running with the ball was prohibited; there were two teams, two goals, a center line, and the field was about 100 yards long. Egede likened it to the "Foot-ball" of his native Norway, which was a kicking game and the forerunner of soccer.

At any rate, the Eskimos outdid the Romans, who, although they played football, did not originate the game. It was among many things learned from the vanquished Greeks after the Roman conquest in 146 B.C. The Roman spelling of the name was *Harpastum*.

It is quite probable, though not certain, that the Roman legions as they swept across Europe and invaded Britain brought the game with them and taught it to the natives they subdued. From the dawn of the Christian era through the Middle Ages, football was played throughout Europe under various rules, or no rules. It ranged from a bloody, disorganized clash of two mobs who paid scant attention to the ball, to a stylized form of pageantry which the Italians called *Calcio*.*

This game was an elegant kind of football in which the players, 27 on a side, arranged themselves in symmetrical ranks and kicked the ball back and forth. It was usually presented in the principal square of a city so that "the noble ladies and the people may the better be able to behold the honoured soldiers, gentlemen, seigneurs and princes." So wrote an Italian nobleman, Count Giovanni Bardi, in 1580. There was more pomp and ceremony than action in the Italian game.

Calcio is the Italian word for "kick," from the Latin *calceus* which means "shoe."

Football played by a mob in an English village, 1627.

4

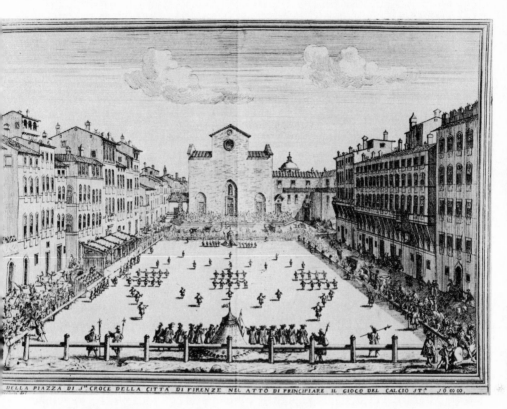

Italian football, *Calcio*, as played in Florence, 1580.

It was a far cry from the football of England at that time. There, no prince or gentleman would have thought of engaging in such a low-class sport as "futeball," as the word was then spelled. It was commoner's game, if it could be called a game, for it was in truth a gigantic, disorganized brawl between two mobs. Often hundreds of youths and men took part in the fray despite royal edicts against the sport.

Shrove Tuesday became the big day of the year for the footballers of old England. On that holiday farmers left their plows and journeyed to town. All business was suspended and everybody turned out for the game. It was town against town.

One town would challenge another and the players, who were mostly farmers, clerks, laborers and servants, would meet midway between the two places. The ball, an inflated pig's bladder, would be tossed in and the mayhem began. Each side tried to drive the ball to the market place of the rival town.

5

The free-for-all sometimes lasted several hours. Often the game ended when darkness fell and both sides were still in open country miles from either town. Football was also played in the cities; the sides would clash on narrow streets while terrified citizens took cover in their homes behind locked doors and shuttered windows.

Wherever it was played, it was a boisterous, bloody affair from start to finish and there were more black eyes and damaged shins than could be counted. But the players loved it. After all, it was the only game a poor man could play in those days.

A fascinating description of the sport has come down to us from 1583, when Philip Stubbes, a disapproving Puritan, wrote:

"For as concerning football playing, I protest unto you it may rather be called a friendlie kind of fight, then a play or recreation; a bloody and murthering practice then a felowly sporte or pastime. For dooth not every one lye in waight for his Adversarie, seeking to overthrowe him & to picke him on his nose, though it be upon hard stones? in ditch or dale, in valley or hill, or what place soever it be, hee careth not, so he have him down. . . . .So that by this meanes, sometimes their necks are broken, sometimes their backs, sometimes their legs, sometimes their armes; sometime one part thrust out of joynt, sometimes their noses gush out with blood, sometimes their eyes start out of their heads; and sometimes hurt in one place, sometimes in another. But whoever escapeth away the best, goeth not scotfree, but is either sore wounded, crushed and bruseed, so as he dyeth of it."

The puritanical eye of Philip Stubbes undoubtedly saw more brutality in the game than actually existed. Nevertheless, it was a bone-shattering sport in his day and players were maimed and sometimes killed.

Gradually, however, it developed into a more controlled sport and less of a town-against-town melee. A few rudimentary rules were adopted. Tripping, slugging, butting and other forms of mayhem were prohibited. In time the sport emerged from the ditches and alleys and was played in more respectable places. Consequently it gained public approval and began to grow in popularity. A century after Philip Stubbes passed from the scene there were football teams in every corner of England. Even the Church of England ceased to frown upon the game.

Football in the market place, England, the 1700's.

Charles II, a sports-loving monarch who reigned from 1660 to 1685, gave football a great boost when he formed a team of his own servants and matched it against the Duke of Albermarle's team. Football reached the upper classes, thanks in large part to his sponsorship.

It became a major sport at the great English secondary schools, which were attended by gentlemen's sons and noble youths. At Harrow, Eton, Westminster, Winchester, Rugby, and other historic schools, intramural games were played under varying sets of rules. There was no uniformity. Each school developed a type of game that was best suited for its particular playground. In the schools where there was not much playing room the game consisted of short kicking and little running. The sides were small, perhaps 11 or 15 boys on each one. Such a school was Westminster, where the playground was a stone pavement enclosed by walls.

At schools where there were wide-open playing fields and plenty of room for running and long kicking, that type of game was played. A side might have as many as 50 players. At Rugby, where football history was to be made, there was ample room for the open game. The field there was known as Old Bigside.

With few exceptions it was entirely a kicking game. Some schools allowed stopping the ball in flight with the hands, or swatting it back with forearm and fist. Another departure was catching the ball, after which the player who caught it was given a free kick at the goal. This was allowed only when the player in the act of catching the ball thrust out his heel and drove it into the ground. This gesture, called "heeling," meant that he would not move or kick the ball until his catch was admitted by the other side. He was then allowed to try for a goal with a free kick.

However different the rules were in the various schools, kicking the ball to advance it down the field was the basic method of play everywhere. No one was permitted (as one written rule stated) "to run with the ball in his grasp toward the opposite goal." The rule was firm. For countless generations no one ever thought of violating it.

But the day came when the rule was broken. It was a sparkling November day in 1823 — a momentous day, as it turned out, for the shattering of the time-honored rule changed the whole character of the game and eventually led to the birth of American football.

It happened at Rugby on Old Bigside. About 100 boys divided into two sides had been kicking the ball back and forth most of the afternoon without either side making a goal. It was close to 5 o'clock, the time when all games must end, according to the school's rigid law. The stroke of the 5 o'clock bell was the signal, and it was obeyed.

Just before the first stroke sounded one side made a final attempt to score by booting the ball high and far down the field. A boy by the name of William Webb Ellis was waiting with outstretched arms for the ball to come down. He caught it just as the first stroke sounded, but instead of heeling the ball and then taking a free kick as everyone thought he would do, Ellis impulsively tucked the ball under his arms and — horrors — started running with it right through the enemy's ranks.

For a moment the whole side stood stunned and motionless.

Then as the boys realized the enormity of Ellis's deed they made for him and tried to stop him. Angry boys reached out for him but Ellis, exhilarated by the touch of madness that had seized him, eluded them by dodging, sidestepping and warding them off by thrusting his free hand in their faces.

At last he struggled across the goal line with the ball still firmly in his grasp. He had made the first touchdown but, of course, it did not count. His magnificent run, which included the first dodge, sidestep and straight-arm, did not result in a score but in a new kind of football.

Ellis was no instant hero. Indeed, he was criticized by many Rugbeians for his flagrant violation of the rules. But he had started something. Some of the players began to realize that running with the ball was more exciting than just kicking it. They tried the new play in their informal games and before long it was accepted and became a feature of the kind of football played at Rugby school.

Other schools heard about "that play they use at Rugby" and tried it out on their own fields. The boys seemed to like the new way of playing the game, which soon become known as Rugby football, or "rugger." This did not mean, however, that the old kicking game was abandoned. Many athletes preferred the original game which, they maintained, was truly football in its purest form.

Eventually the two distinct types of football emerged from the secondary schools and found their way to the universities at Cambridge and Oxford. Strangely, both in England and in the United States (as we shall see), organized football was first played in the secondary schools before the colleges and universities took it up.

What of William Webb Ellis, the frail 18-year-old youth whose feet sprouted wings on Old Bigside and brought new life to the ancient game? A quiet, scholarly boy, he graduated from Rugby and went to Brasenose College, Oxford, two years after his famous run. He studied for the ministry and became rector of the Church of St. Clement Dane's in London. He died on January 24, 1872, aged 66.

His name will never be forgotten. Set in an ivy-covered wall at Rugby, a stone tablet memorializes his gift to football — the running attack. The inscription reads:

THIS STONE
COMMEMORATES THE EXPLOIT OF
WILLIAM WEBB ELLIS
WHO WITH A FINE DISREGARD FOR THE RULES OF
FOOTBALL AS PLAYED IN HIS TIME
FIRST TOOK THE BALL IN HIS ARMS AND RAN WITH IT
THUS ORIGINATING THE DISTINCTIVE FEATURE OF
THE RUGBY GAME
A.D. 1823

He lived to see the development and establishment of both soccer and Rugby.* In December of 1862 the London Football Association was organized by a number of clubs that favored the kicking game. Among the rules drawn up was one that prohibited running with the ball. Ever since 1862 when the association was formed, the game has been known as association football, or "soccer," from the abbreviation "Assoc."

The association became so successful in establishing the game that a group of 17 amateur Rugby clubs decided to form their own organization. This they did at a meeting in London in 1871 when the Rugby Football Union was formed. A year later, not long after Ellis's death, Oxford and Cambridge met in their first Rugby football match.

*Soccer and Rugby have been included in the Olympic Games. Soccer, the most widespread of all team games, has been an Olympic event since 1908. Rugby was listed in the 1900, 1908, 1920 and 1924 Games. Oddly, England has failed to win a Rugby championship in the Olympics. The United States has twice won it, in 1920 and 1924.

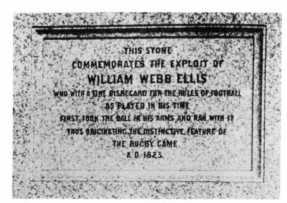

Bronze tablet at Rugby School commemorating the first time the football was ever carried, 1823.

CHAPTER 2

The Game Comes To America

FOOTBALL WAS BROUGHT TO AMERICA by early English colonists, many of whom must have been veterans of the Shrove Tuesday battles in the mother country. The Puritans played football shortly after they landed in New England. There was little time for the game in that stern part of the country but the boys and men of Boston in the early 1600's somehow found the time to stage enough boisterous contests to annoy the citizenry.

In any event, the town issued an order in 1657, as follows: "Foreasmuch as sundry complaints are made that several persons have received hurt by boyes and young men playing at foot-ball in the streets; these are therefore to Injoyne that none be found at that game in any of the Streets, Lanes and Inclosures of this Town, under the penalty of twenty shillings for every offence."

There are very few other references to the game in America during the 17th and 18th centuries. It was not really a game, but rather a haphazard pastime without rules or form and involving no more than one side kicking an air-filled bladder toward the other side's goal.

There was little interest in the game in the colleges of colonial

America. All the early colleges were theological seminaries and the students spent long hours in the classroom and in chapel every day. Between prayers and study there was hardly any time left for recreation.

At Harvard, for example, which John Adams attended in the 1750's, the only free time was after dinner — a heavy meal served at noon — until 2 o'clock. Adams, after he became president, recalled his student days at Harvard — how he used to rush from the dinner table to the playing field and get in a game of football or rounders (the forerunner of baseball). The Harvard boys could not have played a very fast brand of football, fresh from the table and laden with food as they were.

Down at Princeton there was even less time for play. The only free period of the day came after 5 o'clock prayers and ended at 6 o'clock when the supper bell rang. That gave the boys less than an hour for football but at least they played on empty stomachs.

The game at Princeton was a primitive form of football known as "ballown," an old English game. It was fundamentally a kicking game but players were allowed to bat the ball with their fists. They could not handle the ball, however. There was no limit to the number of players and everyone who wanted to play got into the action.

When a large number of boys showed up for a game the two sides were selected according to the alphabetical order of the players' names. One side was made up of those whose names began with the letters from A to L. The other side represented the bottom half of the alphabet. Thus, the A's o L's played the M's to Z's.

This way of choosing sides prevailed when the colleges were small but as they increased in size their various classes tended to become separate units and this gave rise to class rivalry. It found expression on the football field in the form of interclass matches, especially at Yale and Harvard in the 1840's. By this time the students had more freedom and more hours for recreation.

The most bitter interclass conflicts at the two colleges were the annual freshman-sophomore matches. It is questionable whether these clashes should be recorded as football games. Perhaps they were at first but they soon degenerated into wholesale slugfests with every able-bodied man from each class taking part. The ball (a round bladder enclosed in a leather case) was kicked, thrown,

The first picture of an American football game, Yale campus, 1806.

dribbled, carried and usually forgotten after the first few minutes of action. Some years the boys did not bother with the ball at all. They simply went at each other with heads down and fists flying, striving to make the other class give ground.

This furious action, a Yale classicist once pointed out, was strikingly similar to the ancient Spartan game known as *Platanistas,* a description of which appears in Norman Gardiner's "Greek Athletic Sports and Festivals," published in 1910, as follows:

"*Platanistas* was played on an island surrounded by a ditch, between two teams of boys who, entering the ground by bridges at either end, strove by fighting, hitting, kicking, biting to drive their opponents into the water. But for the absence of the ball (concluded the English author of the book) this game bears considerable resemblance to the primitive football scrimmage before any of the existing rules were introduced."

At Yale the freshman-sophomore melees fell into such disrepute that the students were forbidden to hold them on the campus. Undaunted, the boys moved on to the city green and held the games there. After a few years of this the residents of New Haven began

13

The Harvard freshman-sophomore class game in 1875.

to complain and eventually in 1858, the city passed an ordinance against the Yales playing on the green.

An account of the 1858 game was printed in the *New York Evening Post*. It described how the freshmen, under the coaching of upper classmen, formed a huge phalanx "with the ball carrier in the center. Against this formidable mass the sophomores threw their strength in an attempt to recover the ball and push, throw, or kick it over the opponent's goal line. . . . Boys and young men knocked each other down, tore off each other's clothing. Eyes were bunged, faces blackened and bloody, and shirts and coats torn to rags."

The *Evening Post's* reporter would have witnessed almost identical scenes had he been present at the class brawls at Harvard, Brown and Amherst. At Harvard the annual match between the two lower classes took place on the first Monday of the new college year. The day become known as "Bloody Monday."

The games and the riots that often followed them became so scandalous that Harvard and Yale abolished football in 1860. When the Harvard students got the bad news they staged a mock

Drawing by Winslow Homer.

funeral in honor of the deceased football. In a big procession the ball was carried to the Delta, Harvard's playing field, and buried there in a grave. A funeral oration was read and a monument was erected to the ball. The inscription on the monument read:

HIC JACET

FOOTBALL

FIGHTUM

OBIT JULY 2, 1860

AET LX YEARS

RESURGAT

This mixture of English and Latin, freely translated, means: *Here lies Football Fightum, died July 2, 1860, aged 60 years. May he arise.*

The funeral orator mourned in verse:

> Beneath this sod we lay you down,
> This sign of glorious fight;
> With dismal groans and yells we'll drown
> Your mournful burial right!

15

Football at Harvard and Yale lay buried for more than 10 years but it continued to be played at other eastern colleges such as Princeton, Rutgers and Columbia, except during the Civil War when play was curtailed. At this time New England schoolboys, too young to go off to war, took over the game, organized it and introduced a measure of skill and team play unknown on the college campus.

One reason for this was the introduction of the rubber ball just before the Civil War. This large, perfectly round ball of heavy rubber bounced true and could be kicked and dribbled (with the toe) up and down the field with far more accuracy than the bladder ball. Furthermore, it was more durable and could be kicked further than any ball before it. With the new ball came more skillful foot work, longer kicking and better all-around play. The end of aimless shoving and kicking was in sight.

A 12-year-old boy named Gerrit Smith Miller first saw the new ball when he came to the Eagleswood School in New Jersey in 1857. It was just beginning to be used in some schools and colleges. Impressed, Gerrit brought one back to his home town, which was near Lake Oneida in upstate New York, and introduced it to his playmates.

Three years later, when he was 15, Gerrit was sent to the Epes Sargent Dixwell Private Latin School (known as Dixwell Latin) in Boston. He found to his delight that the rubber ball was used there and that Dixwell Latin played football with other schools around Boston — Dorchester High, Boston English High, Boston Public Latin and Roxbury High. These were informal matches but they were the first interscholastic football games played anywhere and they took place almost 10 years before colleges began playing each other.

A well-built youth with a pleasing appearance and an active mind, Gerrit soon became a favorite at Dixwell Latin. He was easily the best athlete in school, excelling in both baseball and football, but it was his imaginative mind that made him stand out above the others.

He realized after a couple of years of playing football at Dixwell Latin that if a team were composed of players trained to help each other advance the ball and defend the goal line it would be

Gerrit Smith Miller, captain and organizer of the Oneida Football Club in 1862. This was the first organized football team in the U.S. *Right:* The rubber football won by the Oneida Football Club in 1863.

unbeatable. Play in those days was highly individualized and boys usually acted on their own without paying much attention to their teammates. Gerrit, a natural leader, saw the weakness in this kind of play and set about convincing the Dixwell players of the value of team work.

To prove his point, Gerrit, in the summer of 1862 following his graduation from Dixwell Latin, got together a group of graduates from his school and other high schools in Boston and organized them into the Oneida Football Club of Boston. He named it after the lake near his home.

This was the very first football organization in the United States. It was a real team and the players on it practiced and worked together at their assigned positions. They were known as "rushers," "tenders," "backfielders" and "outfielders."

The rules of play, which came to be known as the "Boston Rules," were in all essentials the same as those the London Football Association adopted at its meeting several months after the Oneida Football Club was formed.

The ball could be kicked, bunted with the head, hit with the fist, dribbled but it could not be carried. A free kick was granted when a player caught the ball from the air. Holding, tripping and shoving were prohibited. There were 15 players to a side.

The Oneidas played almost all their games on a field on the Boston Common that was about 100 yards long and perhaps half as wide. There were goal lines at either end of the field but no goal posts. A game ended when the ball was kicked across an opponent's goal line. A match consisted of two games out of three. A single game could last a few minutes or it could run more than two hours.

The first diagram of a football formation, 1863.

The Oneida Football Monument and seven members of the original team, 1925.

The longest game the Oneidas ever played went two hours and 45 minutes.

Under Gerrit's leadership the Oneida Club became a smooth well-trained team. Football had never before been played in this country with such precision and efficiency. The Oneidas took on all challengers from 1862 to 1865 and never lost a game during those four years.

They made another kind of football history besides establishing the first long winning streak. The players tied red silk handkerchiefs around their heads to distinguish themselves from their opponents and thus took the first step toward the football uniform.

Gerrit attended Harvard and then returned to his home town in Peterboro, New York, where he went into the dairy business. He proved to be a pioneer in business as well as in football. He was the first to import into the United States the famous Holstein breed of cattle, which came from Holland.

In 1925 Gerrit Miller, a white-haired elderly gentleman but still trim and standing straight, returned to the old field on Boston Common to see the unveiling of a marble monument in commemoration of his famous team. The inscription on it reads: "On this field the Oneida Football Club of Boston, the first organized football club in the United States, played all comers from 1862-65. The Oneida goal was never crossed."

He died in 1937 at the age of 92, the last survivor of the trail-blazing Oneidas.

Football was not played at Harvard while Gerrit Miller was there but it is quite probable that he was instrumental in bringing the game back to Cambridge. Many of his teammates at Dixwell Latin and boys from other Boston schools who played football went to Harvard and they missed playing the game there. They spoke out in its favor. From New Jersey came word of a couple of football matches that had taken place between Princeton and Rutgers in the fall of 1869, and of more games the next year. Football was taking hold, it seemed. It was only a question of time before it would be revived at Harvard — and it was in 1872 when Charles William Eliot, the president of the college, permitted the two lower classes to play a game.

Remembering the bloody conflicts of the past, President Eliot must have had doubts about his judgment when he allowed this game to be staged. He need not have worried, though. It turned out to be orderly and well played. Later that year the Harvard Football Club was founded. Football Fightum had at last risen from his grave.

The aforementioned Princeton-Rutgers games, the first of which took place on the Rutgers campus in New Brunswick, New Jersey on November 6, 1869, grew out of a long-standing rivalry between the two colleges. Both institutions had been founded before the American Revolution and were only 16 miles from each other.

For years the bone of contention between them was a historic cannon on the Princeton campus that was used in the Revolution by George Washington. It was the source of an annual clash between the invading Rutgers students, who tried to seize the field piece, and the defending Princetonians. Eventually the Prince-

20

America's first intercollegiate football game, Nov. 6, 1869. There were 25 players on each side. The score was Rutgers 6; Princeton 4.

tonians sank the cannon in a bed of concrete so that it could not be dislodged and that was the end of the yearly battles.

Why not play football instead, someone suggested. It would be a good substitute and in a way a continuation of the traditional fight for the cannon. Both colleges were playing interclass football under rules that were not too far apart. It would not be difficult to arrange a game governed by rules agreeable to both colleges.

A challenge to a match to be decided by two out of three games was sent by William J. Leggett of Rutgers to Princeton's football captain, William S. Gummere, class of 1870, and was promptly accepted.

The rival captains agreed upon rules that were slightly different from those adopted by the London Football Association. The ball could not be carried. It could be kicked or butted with the head. There were to be 25 players to a side, the goal posts were set 25 feet apart and the first team to score six goals was to be declared the winner.

Rutgers requested Princeton to abolish the free kick, a play

21

that was constantly used in Princeton's interclass games but was not permitted at Rutgers. Rutgers agreed to allow the free kick in the second contest, which was to be held at Princeton.

The first game was played on a lot about 100 yards long on College Avenue in New Brunswick. Some 50 Princeton rooters were in the crowd of about 250. The spectators stood or sat alongside the field. Some perched on a rail fence that lined one side of the lot. There was no admission charge.

Neither were there dressing rooms or a field house. The players got ready for the game by simply taking off their hats and coats. The Rutgers men wound scarlet scarfs around their heads, turban fashion.

There was no levity among the players. Everyone was serious. "Grim looking players were silently stripping, each one surrounded by sympathizing friends, while around each one of the captains was a little crowd, intent upon giving advice." So reported the *Targum*, the Rutgers newspaper.

They took their places on the field and Princeton kicked off. At that instant began the first intercollegiate football game ever played anywhere, including Great Britain.

It was an exciting game, well-played throughout and with the result in doubt almost to the end. Rutgers, cleverly dribbling the ball with short controlled kicks, speedily scored but Princeton came back with a goal to even the score.

"Sis Boom Ah!" yelled the Princeton rooters, thus emitting the first college cheer of record. This was originally the yell of the 7th Regiment of the New York National Guard. The soldiers shouted it in unison as they marched through Princeton on their way south during the Civil War. The Princetonians liked it and adopted it.

Rutgers kicked one between the uprights to make the score, 2-1, but Princeton, as before, rallied and tied the game. Then Rutgers jumped ahead with two goals to lead, 4-2. Again Princeton came from behind ("Sis Boom Ah!") by scoring twice.

The noise, the excitement and the sight of 50 men milling around the lot was too much for a Rutgers professor who happened to be passing by at that moment. Shocked at the scene, he shook his umbrella and shouted, "You will come to no Christian end!"

The professor had no way of knowing how wrong was his prediction. Seven of the Rutgers players became ordained ministers.

With the score 4-4, Rutgers surged ahead with a fine display of team work and made two goals to end the game at 6-4.

A week later, on November 13, the teams met again, this time in Princeton on a field near the present Palmer Stadium that was little more than a cow pasture. In this game the free kick was allowed and the Princetonians made good use of it. Their long high kicks from one player to another which entitled the catchers of the ball to boot it without hindrance for a goal enabled them to swamp Rutgers, 8-0.

Commenting on the style of play at the two colleges, the Princeton *Tarquin* noted: "A fly, or first bound catch entitles a free kick at Princeton. We bat with hands, feet, head, sideways, backward, anyway to get the ball along. We must say that we think our style much more exciting, and more as football should be."

The prospect of the third and deciding game caused so much excitement on both campuses that the faculties of the two colleges would not allow it to be played. They feared that the game would get out of hand and there would be many injuries.

Princeton and Rutgers continued their rivalry in 1870, and met many times thereafter on the football field. But after that victory in the first intercollegiate game, Rutgers had to wait 69 years for a second triumph over the Tigers. Happily for the men of New Brunswick, it came at the dedication of the new Rutgers Stadium on November 5, 1938.

CHAPTER 3

The Eastern Colleges Make the First Rules

COLUMBIA JOINED PRINCETON AND RUTGERS in intercollegiate play in 1870, a year that saw a total of three matches. Princeton and Rutgers met twice. Both games were played at Princeton because the faculty refused to allow the Tigers to leave home. Rutgers was downed twice but, undaunted, challenged Columbia to a match to be played in New Brunswick. Columbia had never played a game with another college and did not have a real team, but the challenge was accepted.

The Lions journeyed to New Brunswick with a team of 20 players, five less than the number Rutgers had previously put on the field, so Rutgers cut five men from its team and the game was on. Such were the casual arrangements made between opposing football teams in those days.

It turned out to be a rough game. Rutgers won, 6-3, and it was the team's first victory after three defeats, all of them at the hands of Princeton.

There were no intercollegiate matches in 1871, probably because of the bad taste left by the Columbia-Rutgers brawl. Football was still under suspicion; college authorities were wary of it.

But the game would not be downed. In the fall of 1871 the Princeton student body held a mass meeting, organized a football association and elected a captain of a team that met no opponents that year. This was the first college football association formed in the United States.

At Yale meantime, the classes with faculty permission began taking up the game again after a lapse of 12 years. The matches were orderly for the most part and were played on vacant lots around the town. The leading spirit in the game's revival was a sturdy Pennsylvanian named David Schley Schaff. He had attended Rugby school in England and had played football there. He was outstanding in the class games and when the Yale Football Association was formed in 1872 he was elected captain.

One of the many oddities of football's early history is that Schaff's specialty was Rugby football, the running game in which the oval, leather-covered ball was used. He sent to England for a Rugby ball and tried to convert his fellow Elis to that game, but he did not succeed. Yale was more interested in soccer, the game the classes played and the one that Princeton, Rutgers and Columbia played with the round, black rubber ball. This was more suitable for kicking than the blunted one from Rugby. So Schaff settled for soccer and he was good at that game, although he still preferred Rugby. He must have smiled a few years later when all the football-playing colleges decided to switch from soccer to Rugby football.

How this came about is another oddity in the story of the infant sport. The move from soccer to Rugby began at Harvard when Football Fightum emerged from the grave in 1872. Although the ball was round and the game was essentially soccer, the Harvards introduced a new play that was a major departure from that game. It was this: the ball could be picked up at any time by any player and the holder could run with it, but only when he was pursued. Harvard, perhaps without knowing it, had introduced to soccer one of the main principles of Rugby.

At any rate, this new game set Harvard apart from the football colleges in the New York area. They continued to play soccer against each other. The "Boston game," as Harvard's version of football was called, was not for them.

When these colleges (Columbia, Princeton, Rutgers and Yale)

sent representatives to the Fifth Avenue Hotel in New York on October 19, 1873, for the purpose of standardizing the rules, they adopted the London Football Association code, which prohibited carrying the ball.

Harvard delegates were invited to the meeting but they politely declined on the ground that their type of game was so different from the one played by the other colleges there would be no point in their coming to New York. In effect the Harvards said, "We like our game the way it is, we don't want to change it to yours and there is no use in even talking about it."

Historians of American football have often speculated as to what would have happened if Harvard had attended the meeting and had been persuaded to go along with the other colleges. The chances are that the football we know today would never have come into existence and very likely our great autumn sport would now be pure soccer. For, as we shall see, American football is a direct descendant of the Rugby game, which was soon to find favor at Harvard.

In the fall of 1873, however, Harvard continued with the Boston game, and as no other college played it, all the matches at Cambridge were between classes. Intramural games were also played at Cornell and the University of Michigan that fall, and these two schools almost got together in an intercollegiate match, according to a story that has persisted over the years.

A Cornell fooball player who corresponded with a friend at Michigan learned that the game was also being played out there. This led to an exchange of challenges and an agreement to meet on neutral ground. Cleveland was chosen for the site; there were to be 30 men to a side (10 more, incidentally, than the number that had been decided upon at the football meeting in New York).

All that was needed to complete the arrangements was permission from the college authorities to stage the match. When President Andrew White of Cornell scanned the written request he thundered, "No. I will not permit 30 men to travel 400 miles merely to agitate a bag of wind." There was no game.

Despite that setback, the sport continued to spread. Teams were formed at New York University, City College of New York, Virginia Military Institute, Washington and Lee, and Stevens Tech of Hoboken, New Jersey. Columbia, Princeton, Rutgers and Yale,

26

the four founders responsible for drawing up the first intercollegiate football rules in America, all saw action that season. Yale played three matches which had significance in the game's development.

The first match played under the new rules took place at Yale on October 25, when the Elis met Rutgers at Hamilton Park, a race track on the outskirts of New Haven. Yale won, 3 goals to 0.

A couple of weeks later on a Friday afternoon, a group of Princetonians entrained for New York and then boarded a Fall River Line boat for New Haven. The students, including the 20-man team, stayed up most of the night singing and frolicking. They had no coach, of course, to interrupt their revelries. The afternoon of their early morning arrival in New Haven the team lined up against the Yales at Hamilton Park, looking fresh and eager for combat. They sported orange ribbons, pinned to their shirts; the Elis wore blue ribbon badges. The ball was put into play, and thus began America's oldest continuous football rivalry.

It was obvious from the start that Princeton had the better team. The Yale goal was continually threatened but there was no score for an hour. Then suddenly came a loud report from the center of action, and all play stopped. The ball lay flat and dead on the ground. Two Elis had simultaneously kicked it and it had burst with a bang.

The game was held up for an hour and 20 minutes while messengers hastened to town in a horse-drawn buggy for another ball. During the delay the Princeton captain, C. Dersheimer, instructed his men on how best to penetrate Yale's tight defense and score. His plan worked well. After play was resumed with the new ball, Princeton quickly scored and followed up with two more goals. Darkness ended the game, with Princeton the winner, 3-0. The Yales gamely cheered their conquerors. Later, the two teams and their followers joined forces at the college and staged the usual after-game dinner and blowout. Early the next morning the Princetons departed on the Owl train for New York, singing, laughing and cavorting — as they had arrived.

Three weeks later, on December 5, the Elis played another noteworthy game in New Haven. Their opponent was a team of Englishmen who called themselves the Eton Players because most of them had played soccer at the British school of that name. By long tradition the Eton soccer teams used only 11 men on a side. Before the game with Yale, the English captain, G. C. Allen, asked the Elis if they would please consider playing with 11 men instead of 20. William S. Halstead, Yale's captain, agreed to the request, and the visitors, attired in natty white flannels, trotted out on the field to face America's first 11-man football team.

Yale was surprised and delighted by the fast, open play made possible with fewer men on the field. Especially impressed was Eugene V. Baker, a freshman back who was to become captain of two Yale football teams (1876 and 1877).

Gene Baker's enthusiasm for the 11-man team never waned and he became an important figure in the development of intercollegiate football in the United States. Under his influence Yale, at the annual intercollegiate football meetings, continually urged the other colleges to adopt the 11-man team. It took a few years to convince them but Yale eventually succeeded, — and it all stemmed from that long-forgotten game with the Eton Players, which Yale won, incidentally, 2-1.

Many Harvard students upon opening the college paper *Magenta* one spring morning in 1874 were surprised to read the following notice: "The McGill University Football Club will meet the Harvard Club on Jarvis Field, Wednesday and Thursday, May 14 and 15. The game probably will be called at three o'clock. Admittance 50 cents. The proceeds will be devoted to the entertainment of our visitors from Montreal." A ticket to the game admitted "bearer and ladies to seats."

Harvard's introduction to intercollegiate football was the result of an exchange of letters between Henry Grant, captain of the Crimson team, and David Roger, the McGill leader. At McGill and other Canadian colleges at that time Rugby had replaced soccer in popularity. But Harvard knew nothing about Rugby and McGill was not familiar with the Boston game, Harvard's specialty. The rival captains, therefore, decided that it would be fair to both teams if two games were played, the first under Harvard's rules, the second under McGill's, which were those of Rugby.

The *Harvard Advocate*, the college magazine, published the Rugby rules so that the spectators (and perhaps the Harvard players) might better understand the game. They were, roughly: the match

28

Harvard battled McGill to a scoreless tie in America's first inter-collegiate game of Rugby football, Cambridge, May 1874.

consisted of three half-hour periods; at each end of the field were goal posts connected by crossbars; a goal was made when a player kicked the ball over the opposing team's crossbar; when a player running with the ball made a touchdown he was given the privilege of a free kick for a possible goal; the touchdown itself did not count in the score.*

The *Harvard Advocate's* comment at the end of the article was: "These rules apparently are wholly unscientific and unsuitable to colleges."

The first game turned out to be a one-sided affair for the Harvards. The McGill men were complete strangers to the Boston game and hardly knew what to do. By agreement the first team to score three goals was to be declared the winner. It took Harvard only 22 minutes to make the three goals and end the match at 3-0.

The next day when the teams faced each other at Rugby almost everyone thought that Harvard did not stand a chance of winning.

*Touchdowns did not count in the British Rugby game. However, some Canadian Rugby clubs included them in the score when neither team made a goal, in which case the side making the most touchdowns was the victor.

But surprisingly, the Crimson team after a slow start seemed to catch on to the game and was able to keep McGill from making a goal. The Harvard men followed the ball closely and tackled well, but they were mystified by the Rugby scrummage.

This formation, which was usually called "scrum" (later to become "scrimmage" in American football), took place after play was halted by a tackle, or when the ball went out of bounds, or by some other development. Scrum was a means of putting the ball in play again, just as our scrimmage is today.

In scrum three forwards lined up with their arms around each other's waist and braced themselves against the opposing forwards who were similarly formed. Behind the forwards and holding on to them and to each other were two more rows (of five players), thus making each group a 3-2-3 mass. The ball was tossed on the ground between the two forward or rush lines and each line tried to get the ball back to one of its halfbacks in the rear by kicking it with the heel. No one was allowed to touch the ball with his hands until it emerged from scrum and was in the clear. Then a back could pick it up and run with it, kick it or pass it laterally or to the rear, but never forward.

Often, possession of the ball when it came "out of scrum" was determined by mere chance. At times the mass of struggling players swayed back and forth for several minutes before the ball bounded into the open.

McGill got the ball out of scrum to its own backs nearly every time, but still was unable to score. Harvard also was kept scoreless and the game ended in a tie. Almost always a scoreless tie in any game is dissatisfying to spectators and players, but this was not so at the Harvard-McGill match. The spectators were excited and thrilled from start to finish and when the game was over they cheered the players of both teams and also the officials. The elated Harvard team was immediately convinced that Rugby was superior to their own game.

In the next issue of the *Harvard Advocate* the magazine reversed itself from its previous stand. "Football will be a popular game of the future," stated the *Advocate*. "The Rugby game is in much better favor than the somewhat sleepy game now played by our men."

30

The Harvard faculty was also favorably impressed and granted the team permission that fall to visit Montreal for a return match with McGill. On October 23 on the grounds of the Montreal Cricket Club before a crowd of 1500 a more experienced Harvard team made three touchdowns but failed to convert them into goals. McGill was held scoreless and Harvard was declared the winner, 3 touchdowns-0.

The Crimson did not play again that year. Meanwhile the colleges around New York continued to play soccer with the round rubber ball, unaware, perhaps, of the momentous strides Harvard had taken toward changing the course of football history.

Early the next fall Harvard's captain, William A. Whiting, challenged Captain William Arnold of Yale to a football match. The two Williams and delegates from both colleges gathered at the Massachusetts House in Springfield on October 18, 1875 to discuss plans for the game.

Harvard and Yale had long been rivals in athletics. This rivalry went back to the summer of 1852 when their eight-oared crews rowed a race over a two-mile course on Lake Winnepesaukee in New Hampshire. This was the first intercollegiate athletic contest

This Harvard-McGill game, played on the grounds of the Montreal Cricket Club, Oct. 23, 1874, marked the first appearance of an American football team in a foreign country.

The first Harvard-Yale game was played in New Haven on Nov. 13, 1875. Harvard won.

of any kind in the United States. The two colleges had been baseball rivals since 1868. And now in 1875 it was Harvard-Yale football, which was to become one of the greatest of all gridiron classics.

At the Springfield meeting Harvard was strong for Rugby; Yale was dubious at first. "Why not play Rugby? It's a gentleman's game," said a Harvard delegate trying to persuade the Yales. Years later, Yale's captain in recalling the incident, said: "He must have been a humorist. I thought of a reporter of a college weekly who had seen a Rugby practice game and he described it as a game for roughnecks equipped with armor."

The delegates agreed to draw up a set of rules that would include the features of Rugby and soccer. It was to be a compromise. Concessions would be made to each game. The new code was called the "Concessionary" rules, but there were only two concessions made to soccer and they were minor ones: the round, soccer ball would be used and only goals would count in the scoring, which meant that a match could not be decided on touchdowns alone.

Otherwise the Rugby rules prevailed, such as: running with

the ball, the scrummage, tackling (above the waist only) and 15 men on a side. The first football game under the so-called Concessionary rules added up to about 95 percent Rugby and five percent soccer, which is just what Harvard wanted. And, as it turned out, this was indeed fortunate.

The Yales went back to New Haven after their diplomatic setback and instead of practicing Rugby they continued to play 20-man soccer, defeating Rutgers, 4-0. The Harvards, meanwhile playing Rugby, rolled up victories over the All-Canada team in Montreal and neighboring Tufts College. There was little doubt about what they would do to Yale when they came to New Haven on November 13 with about 150 rooters.

It was a cold and cloudy day. "It was perfect football weather," one wag later recalled. "Too cold for the spectators and too cold for the players."

Aware of the importance of the game, Yale raised the admission price from the usual 25 cents to 50 cents. There was no outcry. A record crowd of 2,000 willingly paid the price.

The Yale team lined up wearing dark trousers, blue shirts and white caps. The visitors were strikingly attired in crimson shirts and stockings, white knee breeches and caps. It was the first time that full uniforms were worn in a college game.

Captain Arnold kicked off for the Blue and the first Yale-Harvard football game was under way. It was also the first of the many Concessionary matches that would be played as the game developed from soccer-Rugby to Rugby and finally to American football.

It did not take long for the Harvards to display their superiority. They were quick and clever at lateral passing, they tackled hard, and consistently got the ball out of scrum. Completely outclassed in the first two periods, Yale made a better showing in the third but it was then too late. By that time Harvard had piled up a margin of four goals while holding Yale scoreless. Harvard won, 4-0.

It was lucky for Yale that touchdowns did not count in the score or the Blue would have been further humiliated. Harvard made four touchdowns, Yale none. Only one of Harvard's goals was a conversion after a touchdown. The other three were field goals and one of them was a remarkable drop kick by Benjamin S. Blanchard, who booted the ball on the run over Yale's crossbar (a clothesline). He was loudly cheered.

Despite the walkaway, the game was a huge success. The crowd loved it and even the Yale players, battered and bewildered though they were, spoke out in favor of it. They were convinced that Rugby was the game of the future.

So were two Princeton observers, Jotham Potter and W. Earle Dodge, who had come to New Haven to find out about the "other kind of football." Back to Princeton they went, full of enthusiasm for the new action-packed game and persuaded their college mates to switch from soccer to Rugby.

With the "Big Three" (Harvard-Princeton-Yale) lined up in favor of Rugby, other colleges soon joined them. The 1875 season was the last one in which soccer was a major college sport. More than anything else, it was the historic Yale-Harvard game that sold Rugby to the American colleges.

CHAPTER 4

Walter Camp,
The Father of
American Football

AMONG THE 2,000 spectators who saw Yale go down to defeat at the hands of Harvard in the '75 game was a slim 16-year-old schoolboy named Walter Chauncey Camp. The youth was then in his senior year at Hopkins Grammar School in New Haven and he was on his way to Yale. Next fall he would be a freshman and, he vowed as he watched Harvard roll over the inexperienced Yale players in Hamilton Park, he would go out for Rugby and make the team, and he would help Yale avenge this humiliating defeat.

Such thoughts from this slightly built, almost skinny schoolboy would probably have seemed ridiculous if expressed out loud, but young Camp was not dreaming of the impossible. If there was one thing that stamped his character it was determination — and an unswerving dedication for physical fitness.

As a young boy he had realized that he was not endowed with a strong muscular physique and he decided to make the most of what nature had given him: agility, poise and most important, an active and imaginative brain.

Walter liked all sports and he worked hard to build his body so that he could excel in them. His father was the principal of a school in New Haven and the Camp family lived in a large comfortable house on Chapel Street near Yale College. Alone in his room, Walter took special exercises every day. Evenings after he had finished his homework he would slip into a pair of flannel trousers and a sweatshirt and take long runs through the streets of New Haven and out into the country. Only heavy snows or driving rain could keep him from his evening run. He was so persistent and regular on his runs that several persons along his route knew just when to watch for him, and they would wave to him as he went by. He always appeared when he was expected. "You could set your watch by that young Camp boy," they said.

The rigorous training program that Walter imposed upon himself brought him lasting rewards and taught him lessons that he never forgot. Years later, when he was a nationally-admired sports figure, he said: "If a boy wishes to excel he takes on a contract which involves patience, self-control, persistence and hard work. No man or boy ever made himself a leader in sports, or in life, without doing a great deal of hard work which at times seemed to be drudgery ... It is not an easy road, but it is an eminently satisfactory road, because it leads to the desired end."

At Hopkins he became the school's leading athlete. He starred on the baseball team as a pitcher and outfielder; he was a winning sprinter and hurdler; he rowed and played tennis, a brand new game that had recently (1874) been introduced into the United States from England and was already becoming popular.

Hopkins did not have a football team but it did have a large, round black rubber ball that the boys kicked back and forth in the school yard during recess. Walter was easily the outstanding player in these short pickup games. He booted the ball farther and more accurately than any other boy and he always seemed to be under it to catch it when it was kicked to his side of the yard.

In his senior year at Hopkins he spent hours kicking and handling the ball with his friend and classmate, Walter Jennings. The two youths would pass and kick it to each other and run with it, dodging imaginary tacklers. Walter Camp was fascinated by the sport. Although he had never played in a real match, he knew that football would be his game above all others. If these practice sessions with his classmate were fun and at the same time demanding, he could imagine what it would be like to be on a team and play in a regulated Rugby game. Perhaps that fall when he went out for the Yale Rugby team he would find out.

In the early days of college football the game truly "belonged to the boys." The paid coach was unknown — and unthinkable at that time. Graduate advisors hovering about the field and showing the boys how it was done in their day had yet to make their appearance.

The football team was led and controlled solely by the elected student captain (known as the "manager" in some colleges.) He was in complete charge of everything. He made the call for candidates before the season began; he chose the team, ran the practice sessions, stated and enforced the training rules, called the plays and made all the decisions on and off the field.

Such a man was Gene Baker, captain of Yale's 1876 team and a strong believer in Rugby and the 11-man team. He was determined that his men would defeat Harvard that fall. It was Yale's first game of the season and was to be played in New Haven on November 17.

Captain Baker thoroughly studied the British Rugby Union rules and instructed his team in them. He established organization and discipline, and relentlessly drilled the players in the running attack, passing and tackling. He made them train hard. They practiced every afternoon for more than an hour and they ran three miles in the gymnasium at 9 o'clock in the evening.

Yale did all of its practicing with the round soccer ball until 10 days before the game, when Harvard in a gesture of sportmanship sent down a regular Rugby ball. The Elis liked the egg-shaped ball. It was easier to pass and carry than the round one, but they were not sure how it should be kicked — on the side or the end. Baker decreed that the broadside kick was best.

Of the many hopefuls who had come out for the team in late September, only 13 were left as the Harvard game approached. Two of them were substitutes. George Clark and Walter Camp were the only freshmen good enough to win places on the eleven. Neither of the substitutes got into any of Yale's three games that fall.

Harvard was the overwhelming favorite at five to one because of its superior experience, but the Yale team was in superb condition and eager to go at top speed every moment of the two 45-minute

Eugene V. Baker, captain of the
1876 and 1877 Yale teams.

halves. The teams took their places on the field, which was 140 by 70 yards.

Just before play began, Nathaniel Curtis, Harvard's bearded captain walked over to Gene Baker and pointed to Walter Camp.

"You're not going to let that child play, are you?" he asked. "He'll get hurt. He's much too light."

"Go about your business," Baker replied. "He is young but he is all spirit and whipcord."

Walter, who stood an even six feet but weighed only 157 pounds, heard Curtis's remarks. Coolly he looked over the Harvard captain.

The teams lined up with six of the 11 players forming a line of rushers, or forwards, who spread across the width of the field. Behind them were two halfbacks (of whom Walter was one), and behind them were three other backs, all spaced widely.

The Yales were smartly attired in new uniforms. They wore blue shirts with a big white Y, blue stockings, white trousers and blue stocking caps.

38

Gene Baker kicked off to Harvard. Thus began the first 11-man football game between two American colleges in which the Rugby ball was used. The game was of great significance, for it formed the substructure on which Yale and Walter Camp later developed American football. It was still Rugby, but not completely so, for the Rugby Union rules prescribed a 15-man team. Gene Baker had persuaded Harvard's captain to discard that rule and play only 11 men, which, he was convinced, would result in a faster and more open game.

Baker was right. It was a fast match filled with action. Harvard was far more skillful in passing, eluding tacklers and in general team work. But the Elis were tough and persistent. They tackled hard and were tireless. No one on the field was in better shape than the lean, hard-muscled 17-year-old Walter Camp.

Early in the game he saw Harvard's big captain take a lateral pass and start running down the field with the ball, jolting a couple of Elis as he went by stiff-arming them. Walter moved quickly toward him.

The Rugby rules barred tackling below the waist or around the neck. One of the accepted ways of stopping a runner was to leap high aboard him and bring him down. Another way was by grabbing him around the waist or by the arm and flinging him to the ground.

When Walter saw Curtis coming on with his stiff arm outstretched, he knew what to do. With both hands he seized the Harvard captain by the wrist, braced himself, then spun him around in a wide arc and hurled him violently to the ground.

"Well, well!" Curtis smiled as he got to his feet. "You were right, Baker. The little fellow nearly put me out."

After 45 minutes of lively action the first half ended. Neither team had scored. Ten minutes later the second half began and for the next 30 minutes there was still no score. Then Yale advanced the ball to about 35 yards from Harvard's goal line and there Oliver D. Thompson, a sophomore, tried a drop kick. The ball, kicked off his instep in the method popular with Rugbeians, took flight and soared over the 11-foot-high crossbar (a clothesline).

The ecstatic Yales seized Oliver and carried him on their shoulders around the field. An aroused Harvard team fought back

Three action drawings of the 1887 Yale-Princeton game.

1. A fair tackle

2. A foul tackle, too low.

3. A foul tackle, too high.

with renewed fury and broke through the Yale defense for two touchdowns. Twice the Harvards tried to kick goals, a privilege made possible by the touchdowns, and twice they failed. Since touchdowns did not count in the scoring, Yale won the match, 1 goal to 0. The long, hard workouts and the drive under the leadership of Gene Baker brought rewards.

The teams dined together that evening in the custom of the times. They sang songs and praised each other. Harvard insisted that their conquerors were the champions of America, but Yale refused the honor.

Eight days later the two colleges together with delegates from Princeton and Columbia met in Springfield to form the American Intercollegiate Football Association. The meeting was instigated by Princeton.

The delegates were unanimous in approving Rugby football. Gene Baker's table-thumping attempt to convince the other colleges to play 11 men instead of 15 was not accepted. The group voted that touchdowns should count in the scoring, not goals alone as the British rules prescribed, and a match would be decided by a majority of touchdowns. A goal would be worth four touchdowns.

Yale did not like that rule and decided not to join the Association but to go it alone. Baker arranged games with Princeton and Columbia to be played shortly after the meeting. Both Colleges agreed to his terms: the 11-man team and touchdowns not to count. Baker's idea was to defeat all three members of the Association and have a legitimate claim to the championship of America.

Princeton had been weaned on soccer and had never played Rugby until its game with Yale on Thanksgiving Day, 1876. It was a one-sided match which Yale won, 2 goals to 0. History of sorts was made in that game. In the first half when Walter Camp was tackled after a long run, he tossed the ball to Thompson who went all the way for a touchdown. "Foul!" cried the Princetons. "Camp threw a forward pass." "Not so," replied the Yales. After much discussion, referee George V. Bushnell of Yale, who had missed the play, decided the matter by flipping a coin. Yale won the toss and the argument, although Walter probably did throw a forward pass. Many historians regard it as the first one in football history, however illegal it may have been then.

A week later the Elis defeated Columbia, 2 goals to 0. Yale promptly claimed the championship of America and was regarded as such by the Association it had refused to join.

Walter Camp was the fastest back on the team and its best all-around player. He tackled hard and often, he was an elusive runner with the ball and a good passer. (The ball was passed with two hands, basketball fashion, when the man carrying it was tackled or about to be stopped and it often changed hands four or five times during a single play.) Camp was also an excellent kicker. He could punt, drop-kick and place-kick as well as anyone and better than most, and he was cool under pressure. Often when he was running with the ball and about to be tackled he would stop dead and make a perfect drop kick over the tackler's head and above the crossbar for a goal. He did this at distances of more than 40 yards.

Small wonder that Camp had such a long career on the Yale team in those free and easy days when freshmen and graduate students were eligible to play. For six years (1876-81) he played halfback in every game and in the first three games of 1882 when a knee injury ended his career. He was elected captain in his junior and senior years and again as a student in the Yale Medical School, to become the only three-time captain in Yale's history.

He played in 32 games and knew defeat only once — by Princeton in 1878. As captain he was a peerless leader and instilled in his players the will to win, based on austere training and a dedication to physical fitness. Camp would not settle for anything less than excellence, and it was he who laid the foundation of Yale's great football dynasty that dominated the game in an almost unbroken reign for nearly 40 years.

He was a fine athlete in other fields of sport but his real love was football and it was his lifelong devotion. In 1878, the first year of his captaincy, Camp, sporting long sideburns and a flowing moustache, attended his first meeting of the Rules Committee of the Intercollegiate Football Association at Springfield, and from then until he died in 1925 he was a member of every rules meeting and often served as its chairman.

During that time, especially in the game's formative days, his influence on football was tremendous. He was a great innovator and rules-maker who more than any other man was responsible for the evolution of the game from Rugby into its distinct American form.

Camp said little at his first rules meeting, except to recommend 11 players instead of 15, as Gene Baker had done before him. His proposal was rejected that year and again the following year, when Yale joined the Association and reluctantly played with 15 men. At the 1880 meeting, however, Camp persuaded the Association to accept the 11-man team.

This was a big step, for the Association was rapidly gaining in membership and it was recognized by some 25 football-playing colleges as the official governing body. But far more important was Camp's second proposal, which was a plan to discard the Rugby scrummage and use a different formation when two teams lined up against each other.

Camp had been thinking about this for some time. He had an analytical and logical mind, and he saw a glaring weakness in the Rugby game. To him it was ridiculous for a team to gain 15 or 20 yards and then be forced to risk losing possession of the ball in a scrum, from which both teams had an equal chance of getting the ball as it haphazardly bounced out of the swaying mass of 16 hefty players. (During a scrum, which might last 10 minutes, the other 14 players on the field could do nothing but stand around and watch for the ball to appear.)

When a team was advancing a ball down the field toward its opponent's goal it should be rewarded, not penalized, for its efforts, Camp reasoned. It should be able to keep the ball. How could this be done? Camp had the answer. He called the new formation a "scrimmage." It would take place "when the holder of the ball . . . puts it down on the ground in front of him and puts it in play . . . by snapping it back with his foot . . ." (Later, players used their hands to steady the ball and in 1890 the hands alone were used for the snapback.)

Camp's scrimmage gave a team undisputed possession of the ball. The center alone could put it into play with a snapback. This control of the ball gave rise to the set play planned in advance, the sequence of plays, strategy and the use of signals. In fact, almost everything that has developed in the game since 1880 was made possible by the invention of the scrimmage.

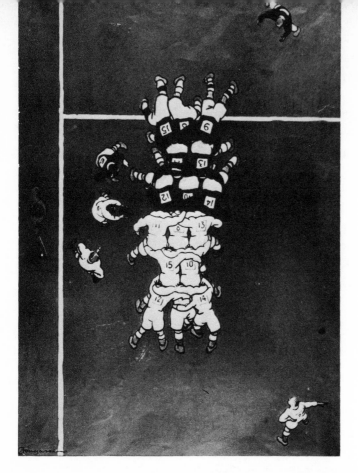

The modern Rugby scr[

Walter Camp will be forever remembered as the "Father of American Football," not only because of his brain child, the scrimmage, but also for the many other improvements he introduced. However, if the scrimmage had been his only contribution he would still be called the Father of American Football, for it was the most important single invention in football, perhaps in any game. American football was born when the scrimmage came into being.

With the number of players reduced from 15 to 11, Harvard, Princeton and Yale experimented with various arrangements of these players in the scrimmage. There was nothing in the rules to prevent a team from having all 11 men on the line of scrimmage, or only the center for that matter, with 10 men behind him.

Camp presented the formation that eventually found favor everywhere. It was: seven men on the line, one at quarterback, two at halfback and one at fullback.

44

The disorganized scrum-like formation of the early American football teams of the 1870's.

The open scrimmage of the 1880's.

This resembled the modern T-formation, except that the seven linemen were spread out almost across the field. Camp later drew the men closer together in a lineup very much like today's formation.

This gave rise to new names for the various positions as most of the Rugby terms were discarded. The "rushers" or "forwards" of Rugby became "linemen." The outside men on the line, originally known as the "end rushers," became "end men" and finally "ends" and the players alongside them, formerly known as the "next to ends," were called "tacklers" because they made more tackles than the other linemen. The two men on either side of the center who protected, or guarded him against a mauling by the opposing linemen (there was no neutral zone between the scrimmage lines) were called "guards."

The Rugby terms for the backs continued to be used. The quarterback was closest to the line and handled the heeled ball. The two halfbacks stood about halfway between him and the fullback, who played deepest and was back of the others.

The revolutionary changes of the early 1880's were significant, but all was not smooth sailing when they were adopted. There was one obvious flaw in the scrimmage and it was a big one: there was no rule that made the side with the ball give it up to the other side. The team that had possession of the ball could hold onto it indefinitely — and that was what Princeton did in its game against Yale in 1880.

Because they had beaten Harvard, the Princetonians believed that they would win the championship if they could hold Yale to a draw. So, as soon as they got the ball in the first half they held onto it and made no attempt to score. In retaliation Yale, having also defeated Harvard, did the same thing in the second half. The result was a long, boring contest that disgusted the spectators — and it was all for nothing. The Association did not award a championship that year.

The following year Yale and Princeton met again and once more Princeton went for another scoreless tie in the mistaken belief that it would lead to the championship. Again Yale held onto the ball during the second half, and the pointless game ended in another scoreless stalemate.

This game was played at the Polo Grounds in New York. The

Walter Chauncey Camp (1859-1925), the Father of American Football, as he looked in his playing days at Yale in the 1870's (left) and as he looked in 1924.

crowd booed and jeered, and many people left the stands before the game was over. The press next day was highly critical of both teams and asked for changes to prevent such dreadful spectacles in the future. The "block" game, as this kind of football was called, might well have ruined the sport had it been allowed to continue.

Walter Camp again came up with the answer. At the 1882 meeting of the rules committee he put through an amendment stating that if the team with the ball failed to gain five yards in three downs "they must give up the ball to the other side." On the other hand, if the team made the required yardage in three downs or less, it would be rewarded by keeping the ball.

This system of downs and plays in sequence completed the basic structure of American football. (In 1912 the rule was changed to 10 yards in four downs.)

Camp was subjected to some questioning at the rules committee meeting before his proposal was accepted. "How are you going to tell when the five yards have been made?" he was asked.

Yale's 1879 team, Walter Camp holding the ball. Frederic Remington, famous artist of the Wild West, is extreme right in the front row.

"We'll have to rule off the field with horizontal striped lines five yards apart," Camp replied.

"Good heavens!" exclaimed one delegate. "The field will look like a gridiron, won't it?"

"Exactly," said Walter. "Exactly."

Camp quit medical school in 1883 because, he said, "I can't bear the sight of blood." He went to work for the New Haven Clock Company and stayed with the firm for 42 years, dividing his time between business and football.

Many more innovations came from Camp's fertile mind. A partial list includes: tackling below the waist, penalties for being offside or delaying the game, and numerical scoring with point values for a field goal, touchdown, goal after touchdown and a safety.

48

In 1885 he proposed a neutral zone between the two scrimmage lines to keep the linemen from slugging each other, which was then the general practice and was giving football a bad name. His proposal was rejected, but in 1906, 21 years later, it was finally made a rule. This shows how far ahead of the game he was in his thinking.

Camp is credited by some historians with originating the selection of the All-America teams. He may have started this practice in collaboration with Caspar Whitney, a sports editor, or he may even have succeeded Whitney — no one is sure — but it was Camp who popularized and established the custom of annually naming the 11 best football players, and his teams were recognized by football experts and the general public above all other selections from 1889 to 1924.

At the age of 65 he was still the supreme authority of the All-America, as well as editor of the annual *Football Guide*, and he was the most beloved and revered football figure in the nation. Late in his life when he was seen entering Yale Bowl to take his seat of honor on the bench, the Yale stands would rise and applaud him.

On March 13, 1925, he left New Haven to attend a football rules meeting in New York. He was his usual self at the meeting — observant, keen and polite. That night he died during his sleep in his hotel room.

Three line drawings of the Yale-Princeton game in 1887 as they appeared in the *Century Magazine* that year.

The line-up.

The ball is heeled back by the center rush and taken by the quarterback.

The ball is passed back to the halfback.

CHAPTER 5

Heroes of the
Early Gridiron

UNDER WALTER CAMP'S GUIDING HAND football was transformed into a wide-open, high-scoring game that featured the running attack, passing and kicking. It was exciting to watch and to play, and it produced the game's first great running backs and kickers, whose feats have yet to be bettered.

Once the infamous "block" game was outlawed, football's popularity soared. More and more colleges took up the game, and it was played by most of the leading eastern preparatory schools.

Attendance increased everywhere. Crowds stormed the Polo Grounds where the Big Three customarily played their key games because gate receipts were higher there than on college playing fields. In 1883 a record crowd of 10,000 watched the Yale-Harvard game in New York. Four years later 24,00 people saw the two rivals clash, and four years after that game 40,000 spectators witnessed the Yale-Princeton annual battle in the Polo Grounds.

Football was not without its critics, however. It was a rough game. The tackling was hard and when the man with the ball went down, the defense made sure he stayed down by piling on and making him immobile. (This was not illegal. The downed ball carrier

51

could crawl forward or continue to run if he could regain his feet.) Slugging among the linemen was common and often blood flowed freely from their faces all down the line on both sides.

"The players looked like men fresh from battle," wrote a shocked reporter of the 1884 Yale-Princeton game. Injuries were prevalent but nothing like what they were to become when the bone-cracking, mass-momentum plays became part of the game in the 1890's.

There were many interesting and significant changes in football during the Gas-Lit Era that were not entered in the rule book. For example, the Princeton team in 1877 blossomed out in laced canvas jackets that snugly fitted the body and made tackling a runner more difficult. The "smock," as the jacket was called, was named for its originator, Ledu P. Smock of Princeton. The Princeton players wore orange and black striped sleeves and stockings with the smock. "They look like tigers," someone said, and the first nickname in college football came into being.

For a generation the smock and the padded "moleskin" pants (introduced in 1888) made up the standard football uniform wherever the game was played. Added to it in 1890 were cleated shoes (first used by Yale) and the rubber nose guard, which was designed to protect the broken nose of Edgar Allen Poe, Princeton's quarterback.

The Tigers were the first to wear helmets, in 1896, and they also introduced an important innovation called "guarding the runner," which started the idea of interference and blocking. It was first used in the Harvard game in 1879, when Princeton assigned two men to run with the ball carrier, one on either side of him to ward off tacklers from the side. The men could not run in advance of the ball, for that would have violated the offside rule, a holdover from Rugby which was still in effect. The new maneuver was so successful that it was copied by other colleges. A few years later when the Tigers boldly sent blockers in front of the runner, this tactic was also taken up by other teams. It was illegal, but it was not challenged and the old offside rule disappeared. Thus did interference become the keystone of the offense.

In this era Princeton produced the first of the truly great kickers in Alexander Moffat, captain of the 1883 team. An almost

Diagram of the football field, 1880's.

330 FEET

180 FEET

GOAL

Breaking through the line, 1887.

The open game of the late 1880's.

legendary figure, Moffat was a dashing ball carrier who could stop dead from a hard run and at the same moment boot the ball 65 or 70 yards with either foot. He invented the spiral punt and changed the whole science of punting, but he is also remembered for his fabulous drop-kicking. He kicked four of them against Harvard in 1882, two with each foot at difficult angles for an average of 40 yards. In the Penn game that year he booted six drop kicks. His teammate, John Haxall, was the Tigers' field-goal specialist. In the 1882 Yale game Haxall kicked a 65-yard field goal from placement, a record that stands today.

Running featured the open game, and ball-carrying was not limited to the backs. Anyone on the field could run with the ball. One of the first good broken-field runners was Princeton's quarterback, Henry G. (Tilly) Lamar, who often made long runs without interference. In 1885, when a field goal counted 5 points, a touch-

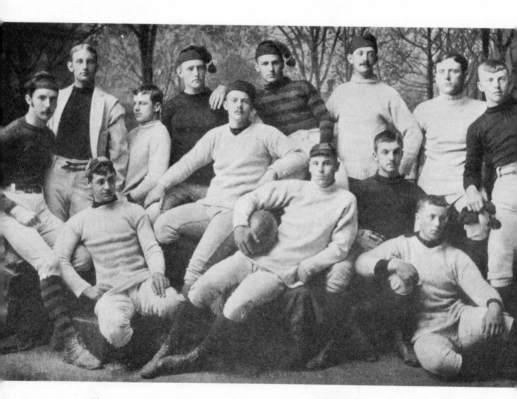

The Princeton 1883 team. Captain Alexander Moffat holds the ball. "Tilly" Lamar (standing) is third from the left.

Lamar starts his famous 90 yard run in the Yale-Princeton game, 1885.

down 4 points, a goal after touchdown and a safety 2 points each,
Yale and Princeton met for the championship. Neither had been
defeated that season. Yale had not been beaten in 47 consecutive
games.

Yale took the lead, 5-0, when George Watkinson drop-kicked
a field goal late in the first half, and that was the score in the closing minutes of the game. Yale punted and Tilly Lamar running full
tilt made a difficult pickup as the ball bounded toward his goal,
then raced 90 yards through the entire Yale team for a touchdown.
That made the score, 5-4, still in Yale's favor, but Richard M.
Hodge booted the ball over the crossbar and Princeton won the
game, 6-5.

After that disappointment, Yale launched another unbeaten
string that began with the next game and totaled 48 games before
it ended — again at the hands of Princeton, in 1889.

The most remarkable run of that era — or of any other time
in the game's history, for that matter — took place at Yale field in
the game with Wesleyan on November 5, 1884. Yale made a
touchdown early in the game, but Wesleyan came back with a long
march and brought the ball down to Yale's goal line. There the
drive halted and the Elis took over the ball.

The field was then 110 yards long from goal to goal. Wyllys Terry, Yale's speedy halfback, got the ball from scrimmage five yards behind his own goal line. The stocky, thick-legged Terry, who loved to run with the ball, bulled through the Wesleyan tacklers, got in the clear and went all the way for a 115-yard touchdown run — the first length-of-the-field run ever made. It is still the longest run on record and may never be equaled, at least not on the present 100-yard-long field.

Terry did a lot more than make his fabulous run that season. He scored 22 touchdowns and kicked 31 conversions after touchdowns.

The linemen were small and light by today's standards. A team averaged about 165 pounds, the linemen perhaps 170 pounds and only a very few stood over six feet. But they were fast and agile and some of them could carry the ball as well as the backs. Tricky plays were devised in which a guard or a tackle would drop out of the line and take the ball from the quarterback.

Even the center would sometimes run with it. William H. (Pa) Corbin, famous "center rush," who was Yale's captain in 1888 and wore a handlebar moustache, originated a risky play whereby he carried the ball from scrimmage. Instead of heeling the ball back to the quarterback, Pa would quickly kick it forward. It was a free ball, of course, the instant he booted it whatever direction it took, but before his surprised opponents could recover themselves, Pa would gather it up and start running for daylight.

He made more than one touchdown that way and also many short gains by dropping on the ball when it bounded through the opposing line. Pa's well-drilled, speedy eleven won 14 games that year without a defeat or a tie and it rolled up 704 points to zero for the teams it conquered. It was coached part-time by Walter Camp, who divided his attention between business and football, and received no salary for coaching.

The 1888 season saw the beginning of the end of the Rugby-style open game and the appearance of mass formations and mass momentum plays which would soon change the whole complexion of football. The transition from open to close play stemmed from a new rule that permitted tackling below the waist but not below the knees.

56

William H. (Pa) Corbin's famous Yale team of 1888 won 14 games and scored 704 points against zero for its opponents. Pa holds the ball. Amos Alonzo Stagg, extreme left center row, became one of the greatest coaches. William W. (Pudge) Heffelfinger, top row third from the left, was an All-time, All-America guard.

During the period of waist tackling (1876-1888) the runner had a marked advantage over the tackler. It was comparatively easy for him to twist loose from the grasp of a tackler. Open field running was the best way to advance the ball.

The line and the backs were loosely spread across the field. The backs got the ball by long lateral passes from the quarterback. The instant a back received the ball he was, in effect, an open-field runner.

But against low tackling he could not break away so easily. He was more often stopped in his tracks, and it became clear that the wide-open game was no longer profitable for the attacking team. The backs could gain more ground by smashing into the line. So, the far-flung line contracted until the players stood shoulder to shoulder, with the backs lined up close behind them.

The Straight Arm as drawn
by Frederic Remington.

Throwing a lateral pass, drawn by
Frederic Remington.

A low runner, drawn by Frederic Remington.

From this close-in formation, which was fully developed in the early 1890's, all kinds of new power plays muscled into the game. Guards and tackles were pulled back from the line to run interference, or to shove the ball carrier through the opposing line (a tactic long since outlawed).

Some linemen had leather handles attached to their backs for the ball carriers to grasp and get a free ride through the massed defenders. If the thrust was stopped, two of the back's teammates would pick him up and hurl him skywards. He would sail over the heads of the struggling players for a gain of a desperately needed yard or two. (This play was not often used because it proved to be hard on the flying back, who sometimes landed on his head.)

Various mass formations, such as the wedge and the turtleback appeared on the gridiron. These dangerous human striking forces differed in design but were basically similar in that the ball carrier was hidden within a fortress of moving players who formed the two-sided wedge or the oval turtleback, wherein the back was entirely surrounded by his teammates.

Phil King, Princeton '91, about to set in motion the wedge.

Yale team in wedge formation, 1893. (The "V-trick")

In the wedge, or "V-trick," as the formation was also called, the 11 players lined up in a solid V-shaped mass with the apex pointed toward the foe. Each man grasped the hips of the man in front. The player with the ball stood at the apex of the V 10 yards back from the opponent's rush line. When all was ready the ball was "kicked off" by the apex man who touched it with his toe (a technical kickoff) but did not release it. He picked it up, the mass started moving forward and the ball disappeared within it.

The defending players assaulted it by throwing themselves directly in front of the mass while others battered its sides and tried to smash it in order to get at the man with the ball. The impact was terrific when the two forces met head on.

The wedge came into general use in 1888 and reached perfection in the early nineties. The ultimate in mass momentum plays, however, was Harvard's flying wedge which was more violent than anything ever seen before and so dangerous to life and limb that it was soon ruled out.

The flying wedge was conceived by Lorin F. Deland, a Harvard fan who was a chess player and student of military tactics, but

60

Princeton's celebrated V formation against Cornell, 1891.

had never played football. He studied the plain wedge, which began with the "touch-off" of the ball and did not have much time to get moving. Deland's idea was to get the wedge rolling *before* the ball was in play, possibly with a forward motion starting 20 or 25 yards behind the ball and reaching it in full flight.

Deland figured out how this could be done and put his plan before the Harvard leaders. They were fascinated by it.

In the summer of 1892 the Harvard team secretly practised the flying wedge on a farm. The players spent hours perfecting their coordinated moves and were ready to launch the play when the season opened, but it was so good they decided to reserve it for Yale.

The Harvard-Yale game was played at Springfield that fall. Both teams were undefeated when they came together and there was much discussion and guessing about the outcome of the game.

Yale opened the game with the conventional wedge but was unable to score. Harvard could not get anywhere either and for the first half there was no score.

At the beginning of the second half Harvard launched the

The original flying wedge. Harvard vs. Yale, 1892.

flying wedge. It was obvious to the crowd as the teams took their positions that the Crimson was up to something. Harvard was not lining up in the orthodox wedge. Instead, Captain Bernie Trafford, Harvard's quarterback, stood alone on the mid-field stripe (then the 55-yard line) with the ball. The rest of his men divided into two groups and took positions at opposite sides of the field near the sidelines about 20 yards behind Trafford. Each five-man group formed a slanting single file. The heavier men were at the front of each file, the lighter and faster men were in the rear.

"This is something new, boys," said Yale's captain, Vance McCormick, to his puzzled men along the line. "Keep your eyes open and don't let them draw you in."

At Trafford's signal the Harvard files began running toward him. They reached top speed as they began to converge just in front of him and at that instant Trafford touched off the ball and disappeared into the mass. He handed the ball to Charlie Brewer, the fullback, who was in the middle of it.

"Sensation runs through the stands at the novel play," wrote Parke H. Davis, a football historian who witnessed it. "It is the most original and beautiful one ever seen upon a football field."

The flying wedge crashed into the Yales with tremendous impact. Orville Hickok, Yale's big guard, dove straight at the Harvard avalanche and got his hands on Brewer but couldn't hold him. Like a human tank the wedge swept on to the Yale's 25-yard line. There, the Yales finally disrupted it by diving low into its flanks and grabbing every leg in sight. The Blue recovered and went on to win, 6-0, but the narrow victory required the full talents of one of Yale's finest elevens.

The new play created a sensation in the football world. By next season almost all of the eastern teams were using plays based on it. The original flying wedge was rarely copied, however, because it demanded the exact coordination of 11 men and was too difficult to execute.

Many variations of it were used and the game became more dangerous than ever, so much so that all wedge plays, flying or not, were banned after the 1893 season. Also outlawed was the token "touch-off" of the ball at midfield at the beginning of a half. Henceforth the ball had to be kicked at least 10 yards. All mass momentum plays were not ruled out, though, and one of the most popular ones was the so-called "Guards Back," which was developed at Pennsylvania by coach George W. Woodruff, a former Yale player.

Four men run interference for the ball carrier in this drawing by Frederic Remington.

In this play, which was to revolutionize offensive football, two guards were brought back, leaving five men on the line of scrimmage. In front of the runner the guards crashed through opposing lines in tandem formation with the force of a battering ram. They went left or right of center and sometimes ran the ends with two blocking backs, thus giving the ball carrier four blockers, three of whom could start before the ball was snapped. It was an extremely powerful mass momentum play and it caused an untold number of injuries before it was outlawed.

Football in the Gay Nineties became a push-and-pull, strain-and-groan game, with accent on power rather than speed and deception. Open-field play was almost non-existent. Slugging with the fist was rampant. Broken jaws and noses, cracked ribs, limb fractures, severe concussions were common. Players jumped on fallen foes. They kicked each other more often than they kicked the ball — or so it seemed to one Englishman who, after seeing a particularly rough college game, commented: "It's quite different than soccer and Rugby. In soccer, you kick the ball. In Rugby, you kick the man when you can't kick the ball. In American football, you kick the man."

He was not too far off. In the Yale-Penn game in 1893, 11 Elis were carried off the field while Penn suffered five casualties. Because of injuries and rough play Harvard broke relations with Yale after the 1894 game, and Army and Navy called off their series that year for the same reasons.

A magazine satirizes the rough-and-tumble game of the 1880's.

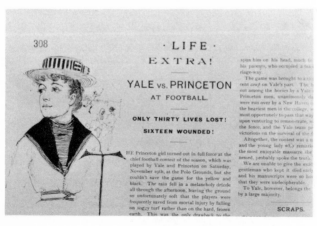

The push-and-pull line play as drawn by an artist more famous for his drawings of beautiful women, Charles Dana Gibson.

The rugged, bruising game continued to flourish despite much public outcry against it. But the players liked the game the way it was. They enjoyed playing it and would not have it changed, nor would thousands of fans who turned out in ever increasing numbers to see their heroes engage in combat.

The first football heroes emerged from the game in this era, the first to become widely known and admired, and whose deeds were recorded on the sports pages of all the leading newspapers throughout the country. Many of these early Titans are still remembered and a few have achieved football immortality and will never be forgotten.

One of the first and perhaps the greatest of the immortals is William Walter (Pudge) Heffelfinger, an extraordinarily fast and powerful guard, who came from Minneapolis and entered Yale in 1888. He stood a rangy 6 feet, 2 inches and weighed about 200 pounds. "He was the fastest big man I ever saw," said Walter Camp.

Pudge Heffelfinger,
the first lineman to
receive national acclaim.

Pudge was the first guard to drop back and run interference around end, and he sometimes carried the ball himself — with the speed of a halfback. As a line-wrecker on defense, the big Minnesotan broke up so many plays single-handedly that he was known as the "One-Man Army."

He stood almost erect, his body leaning forward slightly from the hips, a stance that he made famous, and he would tear a hole in the line with his huge oaken arms and crush the ball carrier.

Mild-mannered and genial off the field, he was a terror on it. He ruined wedges by taking off like a long jumper with his knees doubled up and crashing into the leader full on. The others in the wedge would go down like bowling pins.

Linemen were largely overlooked by the spectators until Pudge came along. He brought crowds to their feet with his exciting play on both offense and defense. In the day of iron men, when injuries were numerous and teams played regulation, 90-minute games twice a week, Pudge was indestructible. He played the full 90 minutes in 52 games over four years and was on the losing side only twice. He made All-America three years (1889-91) and since then he has been selected on every All-Time, All-America team compiled by recognized football historians and analysts. He is the only player to achieve this distinction.

After he left Yale he played on amateur clubs and coached at California and Minnesota. In 1916, when he was 48, he came back to Yale to help whip the line in shape for the big games. In full uniform he scrimmaged against the varsity and, to the wonder of everyone on the field including Camp, he tossed the boys around and ran the ends just as he did in the old days.

In 1922 he captained an all-star team in a charity game against Ohio State Alumni. Grantland Rice, America's foremost sportswriter, watched spellbound as the old guard smashed plays and came out of the line like a thunderbolt to lead the interference. "At the age of 54 Heffelfinger is still the best guard in the country," Rice wrote in his report of the game, which, incidentally, Pudge's team won, 16-0. Pudge played 51 minutes in that game and took part in two more before he hung up his cleats forever. He played his last game in 1934 at age 66.

Pudge made All-America only three years because he was a

Marshall (Ma) Newell, Harvard's four-year All-America tackle, 1890-1893. *Right:* Frank Hinkey, the "Living Flame," was slight of build but played like a demon and made All-America four years as end for Yale.

sophomore when Camp's first mythical eleven appeared in print. He would surely have been picked his freshman year had Camp started his All-America selections a year earlier, for Pudge was the game's outstanding lineman when he was a yearling.

From 1889 to 1924 Camp's selections were widely accepted as the final word. During those 36 years only 12 players were named on his first teams* three years. Rarer still, were the players chosen four years running. There are only four of them and it is doubtful is there will ever be another, as freshmen have long since been barred from varsity football.

The honored four are: Marshall (Ma) Newell, tackle, Harvard (1890-93), Frank Hinkey, end, Yale (1891-94), T. Truxton

*Camp selected one All-America team each year from 1889 to 1896. From 1897 to 1924 he named first, second and third teams.

Hare, guard, Pennsylvania (1897-1900) and F. Gordon Brown, guard, Yale (1897-1900).

Ma Newell, so nicknamed because he "mothered" lonely freshmen and stood up for the weaklings, was a curly-haired, gentle farm boy from the Berkshires of western Massachusetts when he came to Harvard in 1890. He was small for a tackle even in those days. He was only 5 feet, 7 inches tall and weighed 168 pounds, but he was extremely strong and quick. He had a freak build — enormous shoulders and arms, a long back and muscular legs that gave him tremendous driving power. He was in every play — or so it seemed — and his presence was felt by every man on the field. His magnetic personality inspired his teammates.

A natural leader, Ma was a champion of clean play and sportsmanship during the game's most rugged days. He was football's Shining Knight and was greatly admired by his opponents. Even the lowliest freshman affectionately called him "Ma." The press called him the "Perfect Player."

No man ever tackled harder or more often than Frank A. Hinkey, Yale's fiery end, who weighed only 157 pounds in his senior year. "In four years of play no one ever gained an inch around his end," the Old Blues used to say of him, and they would swear it was the truth.

A slight exaggeration, perhaps, but there is no doubt about Hinkey's uncanny ability to nail the runner attempting his end. He did not thrust the interference aside with great strength as the more powerful Ma Newell did, but he always managed to get his hands on the man with the ball. "He drifted through the interference like a disembodied spirit," Camp said of the thin, cadaverous Hinkey, who stood 5 feet, 9 inches. "He weaved through it with a sudden, sinuous glide," said one observer.

He tackled like a fiend. He grabbed the runner at the knees, turned with him in midair and using the runner's own momentum, hurled him headlong to the ground. Often his victim would be stretched out flat facing the direction from which he had come. No one ever tackled or played end as Frank Hinkey did.

To the press he was known as the "Living Flame," the "Silent Man," the "Shadowy End," and to some of his classmates when he was out of hearing, "Consumptive Frank." All of these titles fitted him.

He was indeed a flaming spirit, an aggressive human dynamo in action. Some saw him as a "snarling savage." Off the field he was a silent man, withdrawn and given to few words. "Shadowy" is the right word to describe his sudden appearance out of nowhere to seize a runner or recover a fumble. As for the "Consumptive Frank" appellation, it was true.

He knew when he first came to Yale from his home town of Tonawanda, New York, that he had consumption. "I went out for football against the doctor's orders," he wrote to a friend in the spring of his freshman year, "but I'm not going to do it again."

But he did do it again, of course, — for three more years. He was captain his last two years. He played in only one losing game in four years. That was the big one with Princeton in 1893, Frank's junior year, when both teams came together undefeated. The Tigers won, 6-0. Frank was carried off the field unconscious early in the game.

Was Hinkey really as good as the oldtimers say he was, or is he a blown-up legend? Players who faced him and knowing coaches who had no connection with Yale have said that he was truly among the very greatest. Glenn (Pop) Warner, who coached the Indian Jim Thorpe and Ernie Nevers, both of whom are listed on most "All-Time" teams, said that Hinkey was "the greatest football player of all time."

Yale's other famous end was big Tom Shevlin, a three-year All-American (1902-04). Mike Murphy, Yale's trainer for many years, was once asked to compare Hinkey with Shevlin, a 195-pound bruiser. "If Hinkey was playing one end and Shevlin the other," he said, "no one would know that Shevlin was on the field."

Walter Camp's other two four-year All-Americans, Penn's Truxton Hare and Gordon Brown of Yale, had much in common. Both were born to wealth and both went to exclusive New England preparatory schools, where they played football and were the leaders of their respective schools — Hare at St. Mark's, Brown at Groton.

In college they were brilliant in the classroom as well as on the gridiron. Hare excelled in literature, became an author of eight books and wrote poetry. Brown maintained a better than 90 average and won a Phi Beta Kappa key, scholarship's most coveted honor.

Both were gentlemen-athletes of the highest order, the exact opposite of the tramp athletes who flourished in those days and gave football a bad name.

They were both big men. Hare stood 6 feet, 2 inches and weighed 200. Brown was 6 feet, 4, and about 5 pounds heavier than Hare. They made All-America the same four years but never met on the field. (Penn and Yale did not play each other after the 1893 break until 1925.)

Of the two, Hare was the more versatile and the better all-around player. There was nothing he could not do on a football field. He was a powerhouse at guard, perhaps the strongest man playing the game. He never met his match in line play. As a ball carrier he was better than his own backs at hitting the line or running the ends. He punted, called signals, kicked goals, ran interference and blocked. Walter Camp said that he was the only man who could have made All-America at any position. His teammates revered him. They elected him captain two years.

Gordon Brown was his equal in line play and it would have been interesting had the two ever locked horns in a game. Brown, however, is best remembered as a leader. He was high-principled, resolute and cool under fire. He exerted great influence on the men who played with him. He has been called "the most inspirational of all Yale captains." Under his leadership in 1900, when a football captain had more influence and power than the coach, Yale produced one of its strongest elevens. The team was also noted for its sportsmanship. It was undefeated and untied in 12 games and yielded only 10 points while scoring 336.

It must have been a great relief to Brown and his stalwarts when they faced Princeton in 1900 to know that they had seen the last of Arthur Poe, the Tigers' tiny end. He weighed only 133 pounds but he brought a ton of grief to Yale.

In the 1898 game the diminutive end, who stood 5 feet 3 inches, wrenched the ball from the hands of a Yale halfback and raced 95 yards for the winning touchdown. The following year he made a last-minute, 35-yard drop kick that won the game for Princeton, 11-10. It was the only time he ever kicked the ball in his college football career, which ended in 1899.

Arthur was a member of football's most famous family. He was one of six Poe brothers who played for Princeton. All of them were

The Poe brothers of Princeton. Edgar Allan Poe, '91, holds the ball. Johnny Poe, '95, is at the far right.

small, but every one was fast, alert and full of spunk. They all played an excellent game and succeeded in bedevilling Yale for many years. Two of the brothers made All-America: Edgar Allen as quarterback in 1889, and Arthur in 1899.

The Poe reign at Princeton began in 1880, when Johnson Poe entered college, and ended in 1902 when Gresham Poe graduated. The brothers were great-nephews of Edgar Allen Poe, the poet and writer of horror tales.

As the last century came to a close the Big Three and Penn, which had turned out some fine teams in the midnineties, still dominated the game. Although football had caught on in every section of the country, it was still in the formative stage outside of the East, except perhaps at Michigan, Chicago and a very few other colleges.

The outstanding eastern players were the game's missionaries. As soon as they graduated they were in great demand as coaches everywhere, and they went out and taught the game, often at colleges that had never seen a football. Besides teaching the basic principles of football, they also instituted the rigid training rules and discipline which had been instilled in them back East.

Yale and Princeton, the most renowned football powers of the last century, sent out the greatest number of coaches, but Harvard and Penn were not far behind them.

Yale actually led the field with 53 Elis who became head coaches at other colleges, including such institutions as Notre Dame, Washington, Oregon, California, Southern California, Missouri, Ohio State, Purdue, Minnesota, Indiana, and Army and Navy.

Yale still cherishes a letter that was sent to Walter Camp in 1892 by James H. Kivlan, an instructor at the University of Notre Dame. An excerpt from the letter follows:

Dear Sir:

I want to ask a great favor of you. Will you kindly furnish me with some points on the best way to develop a good football team. I have been asked to coach the team . . . I would welcome any points you might give me. Hoping I am not asking too great a favor of you,

Your sincere admirer,
James H. Kivlan*

Kivlan's letter was typical of the hundreds sent to the Big Three from all over the country, requesting advice on football. No one would have believed then that the eastern giants would one day be surpassed on the gridiron by the very schools that had sought aid from them. But before that came about the game almost perished from its own excesses and would have done so if it had not been for the intervention of a United States president.

*Notre Dame played football prior to 1892 but discontinued it.

The Big Three (Yale, Harvard, Princeton) were the acknowledged powers of the 1880's and 1890's, up to World War I.

CHAPTER 6

The Game Sweeps the Country and Comes of Age

MICHIGAN WAS THE PIONEER football college beyond the eastern seaboard. As early as 1870 the boys at Ann Arbor were kicking a round rubber ball back and forth in a soccer-style game similar to the historic match played the year before at Rutgers. Three years later they formed a football association and drew up rules, fixing the number of players on a side at 30.

That same year (1873), the Michigan boys' challenge to Ithaca to play a game on neutral ground was rejected and they continued to play interclass games. In 1876 Michigan switched from soccer to Rugby and three years later the Wolverines (as the Michigan football team was to be called) played a game of Rugby with Racine, a small Wisconsin college. The teams met on May 30, 1879, on the White Stockings baseball field in Chicago. This was the first intercollegiate football game in the Middle West. The Wolverines won, 1 goal, 1 touchdown to 0.

There were virtually no opponents for Michigan in the Midwest in the 1880's, so the Wolverines decided to go East and take on the best teams in the land. This they did in 1881, when they met Harvard, Yale and Princeton in that order and within six days. They lost all three games but, to the surprise of the East, they gave a good account of themselves. Harvard won, 4-0, Yale beat them, 11-0, and Princeton won, 13-4. These were the first intersectional football games.

Michigan kept coming back for more and took a pasting from the more experienced eastern teams for several years. At long last the Wolverines got together with Cornell and began a series with the Ithacans, who gave them some fearful drubbings: 66-0 in 1889, 58-12 in 1892 and 44-0 in 1893. But the Wolverines kept trying and were finally rewarded on November 23, 1894, when they whipped Cornell, 12-4. This first victory of a western team over a major eastern team brought joy to football players and fans throughout the Middle West.

By that time the game was well established in the Midwest and there was keen rivalry among such powers-to-be as Minnesota, Illinois, Ohio State, Purdue, Chicago, Indiana, Iowa and Northwestern. The South, the Pacific Coast and the Southwest were then playing intercollegiate football but had not advanced as far as the Midwest.

A few schools had taken up the game in the upper South in the 1880's, but it did not reach the "Deep South" or the Gulf States until 1892. That same year Stanford, managed by an undergraduate named Herbert Hoover, met California in the Pacific Coast's first intercollegiate game (Stanford won, 10-7). A year later the Southwest witnessed its first game between two colleges when Texas defeated Dallas, 18-16.

Out of the South about this time came an extraordinary and colorful football team of iron men who set records that surely will never be equaled. They emerged from the most unlikely of places — a small Episcopal college of about 300 students in the mountains of Tennessee known as the University of the South, or Sewanee.

In the late nineties the remote southern school decided to try big-time football. Luke Lea, manager of the team and a born promoter, scoured the South for talented players and persuaded several of them to come to Sewanee on full athletic scholarships. He then got a Princeton man named Herman Suter to coach the team. Suter drilled his charges in eastern-style football and put the final polish on them.

The Sewanee team started the 1899 season with a whirlwind of victories. They beat Georgia, 12-0 and gaining momentum, followed with wins over Georgia Tech (32-0), Tennessee (46-0), and Southwestern (54-0).

The team then left on its history-making tour of 2,500 miles, during which they were scheduled to play five major college teams in a six-day span. They rode in a special sleeper and carried two barrels of Sewanee spring water. The first stop was Austin, Texas.

The game with Texas began badly for Sewanee. Texas carried the ball 80 yards to Sewanee's 15 soon after the opening kickoff. At that point Pop Atkins, a loyal Sewanee alumnus, strode the sidelines waving a fistful of money. "This $250 says Texas won't score in the whole game," shouted Pop. The bet was immediately covered by Texas fans. Sewanee, possibly inspired by the display of cash, stopped Texas cold and went on to win, 12-0.

The boys went to a dance that night in Austin and then hopped aboard the sleeper for Houston, where they met and conquered Texas A.&M. the next afternoon 10-0. That night they made another sleeper jump to New Orleans and the next day took on Tulane, winning easily, 23-0.

After three triumphs in as many days, the team rested the next day, which was a Sunday, and visited a sugar plantation. That night they went on to Baton Rouge and on Monday beat LSU, 34-0. On Tuesday they were in Memphis, where they won their final game of the tour, defeating Mississippi, 12-0.

The triumphant squad of 21 men, of whom only 15 had seen action, returned to Sewanee on their special sleeper. The entire student body met them at the depot, hustled them into a hack and pulled it with two long ropes up the half-mile hill to the college.

Four days later, Sewanee overwhelmed Cumberland at home, 71-0. Next came Auburn, a good team coached by John W. Heisman, a former Penn tackle for whom the most coveted trophy in football is named. He became one of the top coaches in the country. The Auburn game, held in Montgomery, Alabama, on Thanksgiving Day, was close but the Iron Men of Sewanee edged their opponents, 11-10.

With 11 games played and won, and the season ended, Lea still could not relax. North Carolina had played 16 games without

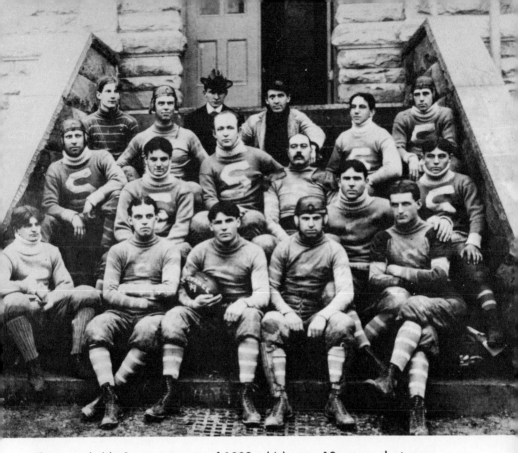

The remarkable Sewanee team of 1889 which won 12 games, lost none and gave up only 10 points while scoring 322 points against the South's best teams. Manager Luke Lea, top row, wears a slouch hat. Next to him (wearing cap) is Coach Herman Suter, a former Princeton player.

defeat in a two-year span (except to the eastern giants, Princeton and Navy) and claimed the "Championship of the South." Not so, said Lea, and promptly wired a challenge to play Sewanee for "the undisputed title."

North Carolina accepted and the teams fought it out at Atlanta, Georgia, on December 2. Sewanee won, 5-0, on a field goal, then worth five points. The winners walked off the field with a phenomenal record: they had scored 322 points to their opponents' 10 in sweeping all 12 games.

Still, at the close of their fabulous season few people outside of the South knew about them. They were ignored by the eastern football experts. Walter Camp's All-America teams continued to be dominated by eastern players. Ten of the 11 men on his first team in 1899 were from Harvard, Yale, Princeton and Penn. But in the South the miracle of Sewanee is still remembered, particularly its amazing tour, when it won five big games in six wonderful days.

The South progressed slowly in developing first-rate teams, although Vanderbilt and Auburn had some good ones during the early 1900's. Vanderbilt came up to New Haven in 1910 and held a fair Yale team to a scoreless tie, then finished its nine-game schedule undefeated, scoring 166 points against its opponents' 8. Camp put a Vanderbilt guard, W. E. Metzger, on his third team that year, but not until 1917 did a southern player make Camp's All-America first team. He was Everett Strupper, a Georgia Tech halfback.

The eastern experts were much more conscious of the good teams that were coming out of the Midwest, where the Western Conference was formed in 1896, later to be known as the Big Nine and the Big Ten.

The first powerhouses produced by the new conference were Wisconsin, Michigan and Chicago. Wisconsin, known as the Badgers and coached by Princeton's Phil King, won the conference championship the first two years of its existence, 1896 and 1897.

The Badgers were helped to victory by Pat O'Dea, who was from Australia and was called "the Kangaroo" by his teammates because he kicked like one. It is doubtful if any player has been his equal in distance, accuracy and consistency in both drop-kicking and punting. His spiral punts were almost always between 60 and 80 yards in games and up to 100 yards in exhibition kicking on windless days. As for drop-kicking, he was good for a goal at 50 yards any time. Here are some of his long-distance scoring drop-kicks listed in official record books: 62 yards against Northwestern, 1898; 60 yards versus Minnesota, 1898; 57 yards versus Illinois, 1899; 57 yards versus Chicago, 1897; 55 yards versus Minnesota, 1897. In practice he once drop-kicked a goal from the 85-yard line.

The East got a look at O'Dea in 1899 when Wisconsin played Yale at New Haven. He was then a senior and captain of the Badgers for the second time. Before the game Pat stood on the mid-field stripe, which was 55 yards from the goal lines, and thrilled the crowd by drop-kicking one ball after another over the crossbars. In the game the Badgers were deep in their own territory most of the afternoon and Pat's only attempt was blocked. However, he spiraled two punts that carried 65 and 70 yards, and several more just below those figures. The Badgers were held scoreless but they allowed Yale only six points.

More than ever the East was made aware of the talented teams west of the Alleghenies. Actually, the year before O'Dea's performance at Yale, the eastern experts were forced to admit that among the Midwest teams there were rivals worthy of the Ivy colleges. The convincer was the game played by Chicago against Penn at Franklin Field in Philadelphia on October 29, 1898. In the stands sat 10,000 spectators eager to see the brand of football the western Maroons had to offer under the coaching of Amos Alonzo Stagg, who was an All-America end at Yale in 1889.

The Penn Quakers were at their zenith at that time. The previous year they had won 15 straight games and were considered the best team in the country. In the current season they were still undefeated and untied after playing nine games. There were three first-team All-Americans on the team. The experts were certain that Penn would win handily.

But to the amazement of the experts and the onlookers in Franklin Field, the visitors pushed the Quakers down the field from their own 40-yard line to the Penn 40. Then Clarence Herschberger, the Maroons' speedy 160-pound halfback, broke loose from a fake dropkick formation and ran to Penn's five-yard line. Here, Gordon Clarke slipped around end and made a touchdown as the Quakers dug in, expecting a line attack. Herschberger kicked the goal and the score was 6-0 after 20 minutes of play.

Penn came back and scored a touchdown, but failed to convert and the visitors were still in front at half time, 6-5. Was the unbelievable about to happen? Could these fast and alert Maroons with their tricky plays keep up their momentum in the second half? The answer was no, not against the far more experienced Quakers who refused to panic. Penn scored three touchdowns, while the Maroons were held to a field goal booted by Herschberger from the 33-yard line. The final score was Penn 23, Chicago 11.

Nevertheless, the East was greatly impressed by the visitors. "Stagg brought out of the West a decided advanced style of play," said Walter Camp. Caspar Whitney, a famous football analyst and

Pat O'Dea, Wisconsin's Kicking Wonder, 1897-1899. *Right:* Clarence Herschberger, University of Chicago halfback, was the first non-easterner to make Walter Camp's All-America first team, 1898.

sports editor, said that Chicago ranked with some of the best teams in the East. In any event, it was the Penn-Chicago game that put western football on the map.

After the 1898 season, Camp for the first time selected non-easterners on his All-America teams. Herschberger made his first team. W. Steckle, a Michigan end, and Pat O'Dea were on his second team.

Herschberger excelled in running and kicking and well deserved his place on the All-America team. He was a fast and elusive break-away runner and was capable of long-range field goals. (He beat Michigan, 7-6, in 1896 with a 40-yard drop kick.)

His fame lingers on in the Midwest, but he is also remembered for an unusual performance off the field. Just before the Wisconsin game in 1897, Herschberger and Walter Kennedy, the team's big quarterback, engaged in an egg-eating contest at the training table. Herschberger ate 13 eggs and won the duel, but immediately suffered a gastritis attack and was too sick to play against Wisconsin. The Badgers won, 23-8. "We were not beaten by 11 Badgers, but by 13 eggs," commented coach Stagg.

In this era of football's history, the full-time professional coach came into being. Many of them were inventors who devised all kinds of new plays, techniques and formations that were later adopted by other coaches.

Of all the brilliant and imaginative coaches — and there were many of them — none has ever approached Lonnie Stagg for inventiveness. If Walter Camp is the Father of Football, Stagg is its Thomas Edison.

On length of career alone, Stagg is the foremost coach of all time. He served an incredible 70 years as a coach after he graduated from the Yale Divinity School. At Yale he was a fiery, 155-pound end and halfback, and also the school's star baseball pitcher for five years. He did not enter the ministry because he discovered that he was a poor speaker and would not succeed as a preacher. His desire to serve youth and promote clean living and sportsmanship led him into coaching.

His first assignment was at the YMCA Training School in Springfield, Massachusetts where he formed the school's first football team and played on it. He was there two years, 1890-1891.

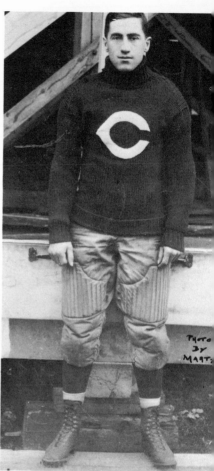

Lonnie Stagg coached football for 70 years and invented more plays and formations than any other coach. *Right:* Walter Eckersall of Chicago made Camp's All-America first teams three years running, 1904-1906.

Then he accepted a professorship and a lifetime appointment as coach and athletic director at the new University of Chicago in 1892. Here too he put together the college's first football team and played on it occasionally for a couple of years. In his 41 years as Chicago's coach, he molded men and teams there that ranked among the best in the Big Ten.

Chicago retired him in 1933 when he was 70, but he scoffed at the idea of loafing the rest of his life. He had more work to do for youth, he said. He rejected the university's pension and went west to coach at the College of the Pacific. He was so successful there that in 1943 at the age of 81 he was named "Coach of the Year," in a national poll of his fellow coaches. He stayed at Pacific for 14 years until he was again retired against his wishes. Even then he still insisted that he had more work to do. In 1947 he joined his son, Amos Alonzo Stagg, Jr., who was head coach at Susquehanna University in Pennsylvania, and served there for six years as offensive coach.

He left Susquehanna in 1953 to be with his wife who was ill in California. The next year, however, he was coaching again, this time at tiny Stockton College in California, where he was an aide and coached kicking. He was then 91 but was still in excellent condition. He played tennis and golf and mowed his lawn. At last he decided that he ought to retire — and did at age 98!

Yale University sent him a congratulatory telegram and informed him that he was Eli's oldest living graduate. The old man wired back his thanks and added with a twinkle that from now on "I will watch my behavior carefully so as not to bring disgrace upon dear old Yale."

Of all persons, Stagg was the least likely to bring disgrace upon himself or anyone. He never drank, smoked or used profanity during his entire life, which ended in 1965, when he was 102. He was highly respected, even revered, by almost everyone who came in contact with him, and his devotion to sportsmanship and fair play was legendary. The great coach was so noted for his code of honor that the Illinois players had no hesitancy in asking him to referee their game with Stagg's own team. He accepted and was completely fair to both sides. In another Big Ten game he asked officials to call back a Chicago touchdown because, he said, one of his players had broken a rule.

At Chicago, Stagg won 254 games, lost 104 and tied 28. He had four unbeaten teams (1899, 1905, 1908 and 1913) and 12 of his teams lost only a single game.

Of the 15 All-Americans he developed, little Walter Eckersall, a 5-foot, 7-inch quarterback who weighed 140 pounds, was the most outstanding. Some experts have named him football's All-Time Quarterback. He made Camp's first teams for three straight years, 1904-1906.

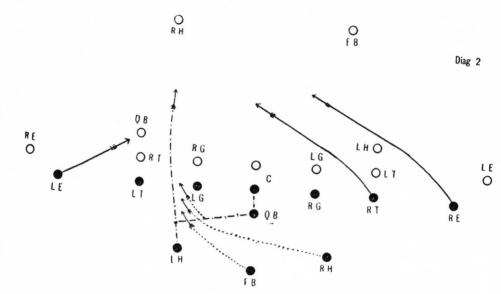

2. Half-back between guard and tackle on his own side.

To send LH between LG and LT, the backs and ends occupy *exactly* the same position as in play No. 1.

The *instant* the ball is put in play, LH, FB, and RH dash forward as before ; LH receives the ball at about x on a short pass from QB, and with *head down* and ball clasped at the stomach with both hands,* dashes into the opening between LT and LG, while FB, RH, and QB follow *directly behind* and push *with all their might* as he strikes the line.

LT lifts his man *back* and to the *left*, while LG lifts his man *back* and to the *right* the moment the ball is snapped, in order to open the line.

LE, RT, and RE also start the instant the ball is put in play ; LE dashes into the first man behind the opposing line, making sure at the same time that no one reaches LH from outside of LT before he strikes the line, while RE and RT take the directions indicated in the diagram, to arrive ahead of and interfere for LH as they go together down the field.

NOTE. It will the duty of RE and RT to block the opposing RH and FB, and each should make for the point in front of LH where he can best interfere with and block his particular man.

---

* It will be a great advantage upon emerging from the line to shift the ball to one arm, in order to have the other to use in warding off.

Formation and instructions from *Football,* a book by Amos Alonzo Stagg and H. L. Williams, published 1893. This is the first book that contained diagrams of college football formations and plays.

"Eckie, Eckie, break your neckie, Eckersall," the Michigan rooters used to yell at him as he scampered about the gridiron like a jackrabbit. He was extremely fast, a holder of several interscholastic track records in the dashes, and he was cool and smart in directing the Maroons. He could outkick almost any of the big players and he was a vicious tackler on the order of Frank Hinkey, another little fellow.

To list all of Stagg's inventions would require several pages. However, here are a few that can be attributed to football's most creative coach:

The ends-back formation; the center snap; the shifting of linemen from one side of center to the other; the huddle; the direct pass from center; the man in motion in the backfield; the backfield shift (from which developed the Notre Dame shift); the use of a flanker for forward pass purposes; the principle of the optional pass or run; the 7-2-2 defense, also the 6-2-1-2 and the 5-2-1-2-1 defenses; the unbalanced offensive line.

Stagg wrote the first book on football illustrated with diagrams (1893), he led the first team across the Rockies to play in California (Chicago-Sanford, 1894), he invented the tackling dummy, designed the first batting cage for baseball (1893), and for good measure invented troughs for overflow from swimming pools.

His talents and high principles influenced generations of youths who played for him, but the headline-maker in the Midwest in the early years of this century was not Stagg, but a coach of another stripe named Fielding H. (Hurry Up) Yost.

Yost was a dynamic, talkative 30-year-old when he took over at Michigan in 1901. A West Virginian by birth and an itinerant football coach by trade, he had also been a deputy marshal in a tough coal-mining town, a laborer in the oil fields and a school teacher. He entered West Virginia Law School at the age of 21 and played in the first football game he ever saw. He was a tough 200-pounder and loved the bruising game.

In the first four years of his coaching career (1897-1900), Yost was constantly on the move. He coached in Ohio, Nebraska, Kansas and California, where he directed four teams simultaneously: the Stanford varsity and freshmen, San José Normal College and a school called California Ukiah. The task did not faze this brash young man. He made winners of all four, then hopped to Michigan, where he made instant history by appearing at his first practice session in a dark business suit, starched white collar and tie. "Hurry up! Hurry up, or make room for someone who will!" he shouted up and down the field, and his nickname was born.

Hurry Up Yost reached back to California for a player named Willie Heston, a fast 185-pound halfback and guard he had coached at San José Normal. Willie had graduated and was teaching grade school, but when Yost summoned him he dropped his pointer and hurried to Michigan.

Under Yost's wing again, Willie became a marvel. He was a compact, powerful runner and an explosive starter. He could beat Michigan's Olympic champion sprinter, Archie Hahn, in the 40-yard dash but not beyond that distance.

AXIOMS.

Line up quickly the moment the ball is down and play a dashing game from start to finish.

Never under any circumstances talk about your hurts and bruises. If you are unable to play, or have a severe strain, tell the captain at once. He will always release you.

When thrown hard always get up as if not hurt in the slightest. You will be thrown twice as hard next time if you appear to be easily hurt by a fall.

When coached upon the field never under any circumstances answer back or make any excuses. Do as nearly as possible exactly what you are told.

Always throw your man hard, and toward his own goal, when you tackle him.

Never converse with an opponent during the game, but wait until the game is over for the exchange of civilities.

If you miss a tackle turn right around and follow the man at utmost speed; some one else may block him just long enough for you to catch him from behind.

Never play a "slugging game"; it interferes with good football playing.

Try to make a touch-down during the first two minutes of the game, before the opponents have become fairly waked up.

Play a *fast* game; let one play come after the next in rapid succession without any waits or delays. The more rapidly you play, the more effective it will be. Therefore

line up quickly and get back in your regular p stantly after making a run.

When thrown, allow yourself to fall limp, w straight, and then you will not get hurt. Do no save yourself by putting out a hand or arm; it sprained or broken. If you are flat on the grou cannot be hurt, no matter how many pile on top

Always tackle low. The region between the kn waist is the place to be aimed at. When prep tackle, keep your eyes on the runner's hips, for t the least changeable part of the body.

Lift the runner off his feet and throw him tow own goal. When not near enough to do this, through the air at him and hit him as hard as with the shoulder; at the same time grip him w arms and drag him down. Always put the head doing this and throw the weight forward quic hard. Crawl up on the runner when he falls and ball away if possible; at least prevent its being pa

When the runner is in a mass, or wedge, drive lift his legs out from under him, or fall down in him.

If the runner's feet are held, push back on h and make him fall toward his own goal.

Don't wait for the runner to meet you; meet the

Always have a hand in the tackle. Don't "thi runner is stopped; make sure of it.

Follow your own runners hard; you may have a to assist him, or block off for him. Always be in ness to receive the ball from the runner when he is t

Fall on the ball always in a scrimmage, or wh rounded by opponents. When the ball is kicked your own goal, or across the side line, do not fa

Axioms from *Football* by Stagg and Williams.

Fielding H. (Hurry-Up) Yost. *Right:* Willie Heston, Michigan's outstanding player under Coach Hurry-Up Yost. All-America 1901 and 1902, he played in 54 games and scored 72 touchdowns.

Yost departed from the standard tug-and-shove, five-yards-in-three-downs system in which ponderous linemen battered each other like moose in combat, and put his emphasis on speed and alertness. Slow-moving linemen were replaced by lighter men who were quick and agile.

His first Michigan team roared through the 1901 season like a runaway express train. The Wolverines won all of their 11 games without yielding a point. They scored 550 points and were merciless. They pulverized Buffalo, 128-0. During that game a dazed Buffalo substitute staggered to the Michigan bench and sat down. "You're on the wrong side, son," said Yost.

"Oh, no, I ain't," the boy said and stayed where he was.

At the end of the regular season Yost took a squad of 13 men to California to play Stanford, his old team, at the invitation of the Tournament of Roses Association. This "Tournament" was founded in 1889 by the residents of Pasadena, most of whom were easterners. The annual festival featured a parade, floral displays and a few sports — hence the word "Tournament."

The Association decided to add football to the list of sports on the 1901 New Year's Day program and this event became known as the Rose Bowl. Thus did Michigan and Stanford play in the first Rose Bowl game.

It was hardly a game. The Wolverines overpowered the Stanford Indians and were so far ahead at half-time that Stanford's coach asked Yost to ease up. In the second half, when the score had mounted to 49-0, the game was cut six minutes short. Even so, Michigan with 11 men (there were no substitutes) had time to run 142 plays and gain 1,463 yards — and this was without the forward pass. Not many of today's teams gain half that distance even with the pass.

After the slaughter the Tournament of Roses Association decided that football should be dropped from the annual program until California could produce better teams. (The next Rose Bowl game was played in 1916, and it has been held annually since then.)

In 1902 the Wolverines thundered ahead at a furious pace. They were unbeatable again, winning 11 games and scoring 644 points against their opponents' 12. The surge continued through 1903 and 1904, although they were tied by Minnesota, 6-6, in 1903. Their record remained unblemished until their 13th and last game of the 1905 season, when Stagg's men with the brilliant Eckie at the helm squeaked out a 2-0 victory on a safety.

So ended a fabulous reign (1901-1905) during which the Wolverines won 55 games, lost only one and tied one. They rolled up an amazing 2,819 points against a total of 42 for all challengers, and they beat representative midwest teams along the way, some by humiliating scores, such as Michigan State, 119-0; Iowa, 107-0 and Ohio State, 86-0.

Football historians invariably refer to these great elevens as Yost's "Point-a-Minute" teams, a title conceived by some careless sportswriter after the dynasty ended. Although it is a catchy phrase, it is not accurate. It is based on the 60-minute game, which did not exist until 1906. Yost's early teams played 70 minutes per game, a fact that historians have overlooked. The Wolverines highest-scoring season was 1902, when they averaged 58 points a game against the 70 points they should have made to earn the title. In their five seasons they averaged 49.4 points a game, which is 20.6 points below the needed 70.

Point-a-Minute or not, there is no doubt about the caliber of those teams. They were indeed great. They were superbly coached and team spirit was always high. Speed was their trademark. The quarterback would start calling the next play while his men were getting to their feet from the previous one. They lined up quickly and the ball was snapped back without delay. They constantly got the jump on their opponents and bewildered them with their speed and deception.

They had outstanding players, too. One of the best was Adolph G. (Germany) Schulz, a 245-pound center who stood 6 feet, 4 inches and had the grace and quickness of a cat. He could play 70 minutes at top speed without tiring. He was the first center to drop back from the line a foot or two on defense, which is to say that he was the first roving center. Schulz was also one of the first centers to use a spiral pass to the backfield.

Next to Adolph Schulz on the 1904 line was a guard named Henry Schulte. Much confusion resulted because of the similarity of their names, so their teammates decided to call the center "Germany" Schulz and the guard "Indian" Schulte. The center became so widely known by his nickname that in later life he signed his checks and listed himself in the telephone directory as Germany Schulz.

Walter Camp, who picked Germany on his 1908 All-America team, once told the great center, "As long as I live you will remain my All-Time, All-America center."

Willie Heston also brought enduring fame to Michigan. The curly-haired speedster was on Camp's 1901 and 1902 teams, and he well deserved his All-America honors. In his four-year career at Michigan he played 54 games, carried the ball 2,311 yards and made 72 touchdowns.

Years later when Red Grange was making history at Illinois, Yost was asked how he would compare Willie and Grange. "Grange is good," he said, "but when Willie played there were no forward passes to worry the defense. Every team he played against worried only about Willie. They went after him on every play, yet he ran 'em ragged. If he played today, why, he'd make a touchdown every time he got his hands on the ball!" This was more than a slight exaggeration — perhaps. But everyone who ever saw Willie play agreed that he was good.

There were several developments in the early part of this century that had a bearing on the game. In 1903 Harvard dedicated its stadium. It was the largest reinforced steel and concrete structure in the world and was America's first football stadium. Yale followed with the Bowl, exceeding Harvard's stadium in size and seating capacity, and Princeton built Palmer Stadium. Both were completed in 1914.

Although the flying wedge had long been abolished, vestiges of it still remained: hurdling, flying tackles, mass formations and line play that often became wholesale slugging matches from end to end. (There was no "neutral zone" on the line of scrimmage.)

A magazine cartoon on college football, 1895.

Harvard Stadium, dedicated on Nov. 14, 1903, was the first football stadium in America.

President Theodore Roosevelt, a strong advocate of vigorous athletics, realized that the game would destroy itself unless something were done. In October of 1905, after he had seen a photograph of a bloodied and brutally beaten Swarthmore lineman named Bob Maxwell staggering from the field, a result of Penn's deliberately dirty play, he summoned representatives of Harvard, Yale and Princeton to the White House and angrily demanded that they use their influence to clean up the game or it would soon be outlawed.

The response was immediate. Football officials were swamped with telegrams that bore the same general theme: football must be entirely made over, or abolished. Columbia decided that it had enough of the sport and gave it up for 10 years. Union and Northwestern dropped it for a year, and Stanford and California replaced it with Rugby.

The assault against the game increased at the end of the 1905 season when Stagg in his annual review of the sport in the Chicago Tribune revealed that 18 players had been killed, and 154 more had been seriously injured. The nation was stunned by the figures. Charles W. Eliot, President of Harvard, observed, "Death and injuries are not the strongest argument against football. That cheating and brutality are profitable is the main evil."

Football officials and college delegates held two meetings in New York in December and discussed various reforms. This led to the historic gathering on January 12, 1906 from which came an organization that later became the National Collegiate Athletic Association (N.C.A.A.).

The Rules Committee, under the leadership of Walter Camp and Captain Palmer E. Pierce of West Point, made some far-reaching changes that opened up the game and reduced the hazards. Among them were:

> Legalization of the forward pass.
> Establishing a neutral zone the length of the ball between the opposing lines.
> Increasing the yardage required for a first down from five yards to 10 in three downs.
> Reducing game time from 70 to 60 minutes and dividing it into two halves.

This was the beginning of an era of drastic changes in football. The turning point came in 1906, when the game started to evolve from its primitive stage and, after about six years, to come of age. The football played following the rule changes in 1912 is basically the same game that is played today. The year 1913 marked the beginning of the modern game.

Here, briefly, is a partial list of the major changes made from 1907 to 1912:

The value of a field goal was reduced from 4 to 3 points, and a touchdown was increased from 5 to 6 points.

Outlawed were: the flying tackle, crawling by the ball carrier, and interlocking interference (a form of the wedge). It was also declared illegal "to use hands, arms, or body to push, pull or hold upon his feet the player carrying the ball."

Seven men were required to be on the offensive scrimmage line, thus eliminating the deadly mass plays.

The halves were divided into two quarters of 15 minutes each; the number of downs required to keep possession of the ball was

This 1905 cartoon satirizes President Theodore Roosevelt's crusade against football brutality. Being tamed in the foreground is "Football Slugger." Behind are Roosevelt's other conquests (*l. to r.*): "Russian Bear," "Democratic Donkey," "Government Grafter," "Spanish Monkey," "Broncho," and "Chinese Dragon."

increased from 3 to 4 in 10 yards; a player withdrawn from the game could return in any succeeding period. (Before this rule, a player removed from the game had to stay out.)

The field was reduced from 110 yards to 100, but 10-yard end zones were created in which forward passes could be caught.

The forward pass was at first hampered by many restrictions but it was liberalized within a few years. At first, the pass had to cross the line of scrimmage within five yards from the point where the ball had been put in play. An incomplete pass when touched but not caught, could be recovered by either side (in effect, a fumble). If the pass fell to the ground untouched, the offensive team lost the ball. A pass caught behind the goal was a touchback, not a touchdown.

In 1910 the five-yard restriction was removed and the pass could cross the line of scrimmage at any point. However, it had to be thrown at least five yards behind the line.

In 1912 the receiver was protected by rules prohibiting defensive players from interfering with him. (Earlier, a player on defense could flatten the would-be receiver with a block, even clip him from behind, without committing a foul.)

The first forward pass ever thrown came from the hands of Walter Camp in the 1876 Yale-Princeton game, as related on page 41 in this book. It was illegal, of course, and unintentional. It was also unseen by the referee, which is the reason that Yale got away with it.

The next forward pass of record was tossed in the North Carolina-Georgia game of 1895 when the Carolina fullback, in punt formation on his goal line, was rushed and, instead of kicking, threw the ball forward out of desperation. It was caught by a startled teammate who ran for a touchdown. Like Camp's pass, this one was unplanned, illegal and unseen by the referee — and it was allowed despite the strong protests of the Georgia coach, Glenn (Pop) Warner.

John Heisman, a spectator at the game and head coach at Auburn, saw the pass from the sidelines and it made a deep impression on him. He had been a strong campaigner against mass plays and he immediately concluded that the forward pass was the answer. If it could be legalized, it would end forever the terrible wedges, he figured.

Heisman, who became one of the game's great coaches, spent many years trying to persuade the rules-makers to accept the forward pass. He was at first ignored but eventually he gathered supporters, including Stagg and Paul Dashiell, Navy's coach. At last, in 1906 "Heisman's forward pass," as the rules-makers called the play, was adopted.

Heisman lived to see the forward pass become the game's most exciting offensive weapon and to feel the satisfaction of knowing before his death in 1936 that he would be forever remembered as the "Father of the Forward Pass." He is also remembered for what his Georgia Tech team did to little Cumberland College of Kentucky on the afternoon of October 17, 1916. Tech poured across an incredible 32 touchdowns and got 30 extra points kicking in four 12½-minute quarters. Cumberland gained 30 yards rushing and did not make a first down. Tech did not punt or pass during the game. The final score: Georgia Tech 222, Cumberland 0. It is the highest score ever recorded in college football.

We have seen who threw the early (and illegal) forward passes, but who tossed the first legal one? The answer is not quite clear. However, we do know that the play was first used legally in a little-known game in 1905 between two small Kansas colleges: Fairmont (now the University of Wichita) and Washburn.

It came about this way: President Roosevelt in his meeting with the Eastern Big Three in midseason suggested that the forward pass be legalized immediately and used in the closing stages of the 1905 season. But the major colleges decided to wait until next year.

Fairmont and Washburn did not want to wait, however. They agreed to meet in a post-season game and try out the pass provided the rules committee would grant them permission to use it. Wires were sent to Walter Camp, who, following a meeting of the rules-makers in early December told the two Kansas colleges to go ahead with their plans. The teams agreed to play on Christmas Day and both began practicing the forward pass. They had two weeks to go.

There is no doubt that the first legal forward pass was thrown in this now-forgotten game, but who threw it or which team initiated it will never be known. Both colleges claim the honor. Old press reports do verify the fact that forward passes were used by both teams but, oddly enough, they fail to say who actually tossed the first one.

In any event, we learn that Hugh Hope, the Washburn quarterback, completed three passes to halfback Glenn Millice for a total of 25 yards, and Bill Davis, Fairmont's captain, completed two for a total of 15 yards. Both passers threw the ball underhand and it floated forward end over end. Neither team scored during the game.

Most football historians are not aware of the Fairmont-Washburn game and the few who are generally ignore it on the grounds that the forward pass rule was not officially entered in the rules book until January 12, 1906. They maintain — and with some justification — that the first legal pass was thrown on September 5, 1906, when Bradbury Robinson, a St. Louis University halfback, tossed the ball forward to his running-mate, Jack Schneider, in a game with Carroll College of Waukesha, Wisconsin.

The St. Louis team was the first one to make full use of the new pass rule. It was coached by Edward B. Cochems, who was years ahead of his contemporaries in adopting the new-fangled weapon.

He prepared for the 1906 season by taking his entire squad to Lake Beulah in Wisconsin for the two summer months. There, he studied the proportions of the clumsy, melon-shaped ball, which players called the "blimp", and realized that it had been designed for kicking and carrying, not for passing. He saw that the lacing was the only part of the ball that allowed finger purchase for throwing on its long axis. Before the first practice he told his players to put their fingers on the lacings nearest the end of the ball and throw it overhand with a twist of the wrist.

Eddie Cochems found an apt pupil in the 6-foot, 4-inch Brad Robinson, who had a buggy-whip arm. In an early practice session Robinson, all excited, ran up to Cochems and said, "Coach, I can throw the darn thing 40 yards." His target was Jack Schneider and they worked together the rest of the summer. Cochems and his players could hardly wait for the season to begin.

What they did that fall stood the football world on its head. The slick Robinson-Schneider combination gave a perfect demon-victims were Iowa (39-0) and Kansas (34-2). Against Kansas, Brad would shoot the ball hard and accurately to Jack Schneider at distances up to 50 yards. Opposing teams became panic-stricken as they stood helplessly watching long passes spiral over their heads for touchdowns. The defenders did not know what to do. When they dropped back to cover Schneider, the St. Louis backs darted through the line or around ends for long gains. Even the officials working the St. Louis games were stunned. One referee said that he had officiated at games around the country and had never seen anything like the St. Louis pass plays.

The team raced through an undefeated season, winning 11 games and scoring 402 points while yielding only 11. Among its victims were Iowa (39-0) and Kansas (34-2). Against Kansas, Brad pitched 48- and 45-yard passes. (Eddie Cochems also turned out fine teams in 1907 and 1908.)

The wonder of it all was that other coaches did not immediately take up the pass and do with it what St. Louis had done. Perhaps it was because St. Louis was a relatively obscure school deep in mid-America, outside of the Big Ten and far from the eastern seaboard, where the game had reached its highest development.

Little attention was paid to the pass in the East even though Yale beat Harvard with it in the 1906 game when halfback Paul Veeder lofted a 35-yard pass to Clarence Alcott, the right end, who caught it three yards from Harvard's goal line and was promptly downed. Moments later Yale scored the only touchdown of the game to win, 6-0. Navy beat Army, that year, 10-0, also by means of the pass.

In general, the East looked upon the pass with mild contempt — something not quite manly, like smashing the line. Furthermore, it carried severe penalties and was not worthwhile. The East could win games without it, so why use it? And anyway, the new play was a fad and would soon die out. So thought the East, with the exception of a few coaches. Pop Warner, Carlisle's coach, was one of the few.

The blunt, egg-shaped ball of 1912 was good for drop-kicking and carrying but not for forward passing. *Right:* The modern ball designed for forward passing.

Coach Stagg was ready for the 1906 season. He created 64 different pass patterns and had his team practice them, but he did not use them much that year. In 1907 and 1908, however, Chicago won the Big Ten championship largely through the use of the many intricate pass patterns that Stagg originated.

Not until 1913 did the forward pass attract national attention and at last convince the East that it was here to stay. The convincer was Notre Dame's upset victory over Army at West Point, gained largely by passes thrown by quarterback Gus Dorais to Knute Rockne and other receivers. The fleet-footed Rockne was captain and left end of the Irish eleven.

The game was played on November 1, 1913 and was the first meeting of the two schools. The Irish were held lightly by the Army, then an eastern power on a par with the Big Three. The Cadets looked upon the game as a friendly warm-up for their annual battle with the Navy. Admission was free, as were all football games at West Point in those days, and only 3,000 spectators sat in the wooden stands.

The Army did not know that Rockne and Dorais, a skinny 145-pounder, had spent the whole previous summer practicing forward passing on the beach at Cedar Point, on Lake Erie, where they worked as restaurant checkers. Daily for hours Gus would throw the ball from all angles to Knute, who ran along the beach dodging imaginary pursuers. At the end of the summer they were a smooth-working, coordinated pair.

Jesse Harper, Notre Dame's coach, watched them perform in the early practice sessions that fall and saw that they were going to be of great value to the team. The Irish eleven that took the field against Army was big and fast, and it centered around the accurate, bullet-like passing of Gus Dorais.

Lightning did not strike immediately, but the first quarter was not very old when Gus on third down suddenly shot a 20-yard pass diagonally across the field to Knute, who took the ball over his shoulder and coasted to the goal line.

Army's heavier line paved the way for two touchdowns, but Notre Dame bounced back with a series of passes and scored again. At the half it was Notre Dame 14, Army 13.

The third quarter was a standoff, but in the final quarter Dorais opened up and passed the Army dizzy. His targets were Rockne, left halfback Joe Pliska and Fred Gushurst, the right end. He got to them at distances from five yards up to 40 yards and completely confounded Army's defense. Cleverly, he mixed his passing attack with line smashes and end runs. The Irish made three touchdowns in the last quarter, all of them the result of passes, and won the game, 35-13.

Little Gus had quite an afternoon. He threw 17 passes, completing 13, and had no interceptions. He gained 243 yards through the air. His toe was as good as his arm. Gus kicked a goal after each of the team's five touchdowns.

Football writer Harry Cross reported the game in the *New York Times* and said, that the "Army's style of old-fashioned, close, line-smashing play was no match for the spectacular and highly perfected attack of the Indiana collegians . . . Football men marveled at this startling display of open football."

Coaches and football observers in the East also marveled at Notre Dame's performance when they read about it the next day. Many sat down with pencil and paper and began diagramming new forward pass patterns. But it took time and tedious work to develop a pass attack, and it required highly skilled players to execute it. The change did not come overnight, but the Irish had pointed the way.

As Knute Rockne said many years after the historic game: "Although we were not the first to use the forward pass, it can truthfully be said that we were among the first to learn how it should be used."

Brad Robinson and Jack Schneider, of course, were the very first to use it effectively, and they played when Knute Rockne and Gus Dorais were 15-year-old schoolboys. But the Irish combination gave the pass its greatest impetus by defeating an eastern power on its own grounds.

Notre Dame in 1913, incidentally, was not the tiny, unknown college that imaginative football writers have so often described it to be. The Irish, in fact, had for years met and held their own against Big Ten opposition. They beat mighty Michigan, 11-3, in 1909, and they had used the forward pass years before they met Army.

There is an interesting sequel to the Notre Dame-Army game.

The Irish went through the 1912 and 1913 seasons undefeated and became nationally known as a first-rate team. As a result, several eastern colleges sought them as an opponent for the 1914 season. Jesse Harper, Notre Dame's coach, accepted a bid from Yale to play in New Haven. His assistant was Knute Rockne.

The Elis were coached by Frank Hinkey, the old Yale end, and their days of glory were behind them. They had not had an undefeated season (or even a Big Three championship) since 1909 and they would not have another one until 1923. Many thought that the Irish with their advanced style of play would humble the fading Blue.

The Irish thought so, and were cocky about it. They came to New Haven with a winning streak of 27 consecutive games and with the Midwest rooting for them. The *New York Times* commented that the "famous eleven is confident of sweeping the Elis off their feet and establishing themselves in the front rank of football society."

Hinkey got a wire from the Chicago Yale Club saying that "everybody in the Midwest is betting Notre Dame upsets Yale," and to please do something about it. He did, and in an unusual way.

He prepared his team by bringing the Hamilton (Ontario) Tigers to New Haven to teach the backfield the lateral passing game of Canadian Rugby, the idea being to surprise the Irish with something new. The Yale backs were fast and they became adept at flipping the ball back and forth.

The outstanding player of the game was Ray Eichenlaub, Notre Dame's big fullback who had demolished the Cadet line the year before. He gained more than 300 yards against Yale, but the Blue line stopped his drives when it counted and held the Irish scoreless. Meanwhile, Yale's use of the lateral was something the westerners had never before encountered.

Rockne tells about it in his autobiography, as follows: "They (the Yale backs) made Notre Dame look like a high-school squad. They lateral-passed Notre Dame out of the park and knocked our ears down to the tune of 28 to 0 — the most valuable lesson Notre Dame ever had in football. It taught us never to be cocksure. Modern football at Notre Dame can be dated from that game, as we made vital use of every lesson we learned.

"On the following Monday, Jesse Harper put in Stagg's back-field shift with my idea of flexing or shuttling the ends, which was the beginning of what is known in football today as the Notre Dame system."

How well Rockne absorbed his lesson is emblazoned in the record books. He became head coach in 1918 and founded the Notre Dame football dynasty. He was football's "winningest" coach and perhaps its most magnetic personality. In his 13 years at the helm of Notre Dame, his teams won 105 games, lost 12 and tied 5. His winning percentage of .881 heads the long list of the game's leading coaches since the 1890's.

Until the 1906 reforms, Harvard, although it had produced some championship teams, had been the least successful of the Big Three. But the Crimson's fortunes changed abruptly with the advent of Percy Duncan Haughton, Harvard's first paid coach.

A product of the exclusive Groton School and Harvard (class of 1899), Haughton was a Boston blue blood, an exceptional athlete, a disciplinarian and a perfectionist. He made Camp's second All-America team as a tackle in 1898, was captain of the Harvard base-ball team his senior year, and became racquets champion of the United States in 1906.

There was no doubt about who was going to be boss when he returned to Harvard to coach in 1908. In a pre-season practice session the team's star fullback came ambling on to the field an hour late. "You," roared Percy, "you get the hell off the field and don't come back." He made it stick, too.

Haughton was the first coach to go in for big squads. He used to exhibit three full elevens before a game and have them go through signals to impress his opponents. He built up what became known as the "Haughton system," which was based on precision, deception and his own absolute authority.

Haughton had a lot more than big squads going for him. He also had quality, and he made the most of it. He had Eddie Mahan, the best broken-field runner of his time, and he had Charlie Brickley, who booted Harvard to many victories with his educated toe and could smash a line with the best of them. And he had Huntington (Tack) Hardwick, an all-around athlete of remarkable ability who, as a team player and leader, was the best of the lot.

Percy Haughton, Harvard's most successful coach. *Right:* Haughton's greatest players: Charlie Brickley, Tack Hardwick and Eddie Mahan.

Brickley and Hardwick entered Harvard in the fall of 1911 and formed the nucleus of Harvard's most famous athletic class (1915) that produced many All-Americans and skilled performers in all sports.

Tack, who earned his nickname because he liked to sail and enjoyed eating hardtack, had much in common with his football coach. Like Haughton, he was a Boston blue blood, a Groton graduate, highly competitive and tough physically. The New England adage, "When Grotons are tough, they are tough," applied to both.

Tack stood an even six feet and weighed about 175 pounds. He was Harvard's strongest man, winner of Dr. Dudley A. Sargent's strength test with a record number of points, and he starred for three years on Harvard's baseball team as an outfielder. He captained it in 1915 and led his team in batting with a .357 average. He was a tournament tennis player, a strong oarsman and liked to put the gloves on and box for the sheer joy of combat. Grantland Rice believed that Tack could have been a champion if he had entered the prize ring.

In football he was Mr. Everything — a tough blocker and tackler without peer, a standout at end or halfback, an elusive ball carrier, a powerful line smasher, a passer and pass receiver and an exceptional place-kicker.

"He could star in any position," said Walter Camp. "The most valuable player in the history of Harvard football," said Haughton. Grantland Rice continually spoke of Tack's "flaming spirit."

The Crimson had a miserable record against Yale when Haughton took over in 1908. In the six previous seasons Yale had won every game and had kept Harvard scoreless. Haughton immediately put an end to the losing streak by beating Yale, 4-0. The next year the Blue came back with an 8-0 victory, then came two scoreless games (1910-1911), followed by four straight wins for Harvard.

Haughton's 1910, 1912 and 1913 teams were rated the best in the nation. In the 1913 Yale game Brickley booted five field goals (dropkicks from the 35-, 38-, 32-, and 24-yard lines and a placement from the 40) for every Harvard point and a 15-5 win. It was the Crimson's first victory over Yale in the Harvard Stadium.

Haughton gave Harvard its longest undefeated cycle: 33 games, from the eighth game in 1911 to the fifth game in 1915, when Cornell finally snapped the streak, 10-0. That was the only losing game that Captain Eddie Mahan played in during his brilliant career at Harvard as a three-year All-America halfback.

In Haughton's first year as coach at Harvard, the Carlisle Indians came to Cambridge for their 12th meeting with the Crimson. The series had started back in 1896, only two years after Carlisle put its first football team on the field. The colorful and often unpredictable Indians had always put on a good show against Harvard and the crowds loved them. The year before they had beaten Harvard, 23-15.

The Industrial School for Indians at Carlisle, Pennsylvania, was the United States government's official title of the school the Indians represented. It was not a college. It was a vocational school for

Indian children and young people of both sexes, who came from many reservations to learn trades, such as tailoring, carpentry and stenography. Many of them worked on farms around Carlisle.

The enrollment was about 1,000, of which there were perhaps 250 youngsters of football age. From this small group came some of the most fabulous teams ever to appear on the football scene. They defeated leading football powers with student bodies more than 10 times larger to draw upon and with football traditions going back many years before the little school ever saw a football. Among the football scalps collected by the Indians were: Penn, Penn State, Ohio State, Army, Navy, Syracuse, Pitt, Nebraska, Alabama, Chicago, Northwestern, Cornell and Minnesota. And the Redmen beat them with teams that never averaged over 170 pounds and with no more than three or four substitutes.

How did they do it? Pop Warner, their creative coach who developed new formations and used many trick plays, said that the Indians were born lovers of sport and had highly developed powers of observation inherited through many generations. They had great speed and skill in the use of hands and feet and they loved combat. Above all, they had fierce pride in their heritage. They wanted to show that in a contest waged on equal terms with the palefaces, they were superior to them. This had never been possible in warfare because of the white man's superior weapons. But on the gridiron the odds were even.

Pop was the perfect coach for them. When he arrived at Carlisle in 1903 he soon realized that the Redmen would not accept criticism or punishment from a white man for mistakes made on the field. The shrewd coach installed a system whereby the players spanked each other for their own mistakes. The Indians delighted in this new treatment that made punishment a game in itself, and Pop gained their admiration.

As for trick plays, Pop was a master of the art and the Indians loved to pull them off to beat the paleface at his own game. One of his best was revealed at the start of the second half in the 1903 game with Harvard when the Crimson kicked off.

The ball was caught by Jimmy Johnson, Carlisle's quarterback, and his mates quickly formed a wedge around him to hide the play. Charley Dillon, a fleet back, crouched down and as he did so

nn (Pop) Warner, Cornell, 1894.

Johnson quickly shoved the ball inside the back of Dillon's jersey, which had an elastic band around the bottom. The wedge broke up and the whole team fanned out in a long line and ran down the field with their arms spread out and palms up as if to say, "Who has the ball?" The Harvards were bewildered, but the crowd could see the lump in Dillon's jersey and there were roars of laughter. Dillon crossed the goal line, pulled the ball from under his jersey, placed it on the ground and sat on it. Pop nearly fell off the bench laughing.

Harvard protested the play but the touchdown was allowed. Later, however, the so-called "hidden ball" play was declared illegal under the sportsmanship rule. In defending his trickery, Pop said, "The public expects the Indians to employ trickery and we try to oblige."

In 1908 Carlisle upset a strong Syracuse team through a ruse devised by Pop. He had pads sewn on the front of the jerseys of his ends and backs in the exact shape and color of a football. By pretending to hold footballs the Redmen confused the Syracuse team and won the game.

Later that season Pop brought his Indians to Cambridge. Haughton had heard about the trickery at Syracuse and the night before the game he talked to Pop about it. "I hope you're not going to try any of that stuff on us," he said.

"Oh, I don't know," Pop replied airily. "There's nothing in the rules that says we can't."

Next day when the coaches met on the field just before the game, Haughton asked Pop to come over to the Harvard bench and select the game ball. The Harvard manager opened a sack of footballs and strewed them on the ground. Every one of them had been dyed crimson, the color of the Harvard jerseys. "You win, Percy," said Pop, and walked across the field shaking his head.

On the field that afternoon, playing his first full season as Carlisle's starting halfback was Jim Thorpe, the magnificent Sac and Fox Indian who was probably the best football player in the game's history. At least, the Associated Press thought so, when 391 sportswriters and broadcasters were polled in 1950 to determine the greatest football player of the first half of the 20th century. Thorpe won with 170 votes to 138 for Red Grange. No one else was close. In addition, Jim won another A.P. poll for the greatest male athlete in all sports, amateur or professional. In this one he topped Babe Ruth, his closest rival, 875 to 539. In a third poll to determine the greatest track and field athlete, Jim ran second to Jesse Owens, the sprinter and long jumper who won four gold medals for the United States in the 1936 Olympic Games.

In the 1912 Olympics at Stockholm, Sweden, the graceful Indian won the pentathlon and the decathlon to become the only athlete ever to win both of these strenuous tests of endurance and skill. In the five-event pentathlon he won four of the five events, and his score was twice that of his nearest rival. In the decathlon he won four of the 10 events. The King of Sweden awarded him special trophies and said, "You, sir, are the greatest athlete in the world."

Jim was also a major-league baseball player but he was not outstanding in this role. He was good enough to play for eight years, however, and in his last season (1919) playing in the outfield for the Boston Braves, he batted .327.

He was, indeed, the athletic marvel of his age. He had a symmetrically proportioned body and was deep through the chest, but none of his measurements were particularly large. He was an inch short of six feet and he weighed about 180 pounds at the peak of his career.

If Jim had never done anything but play football he would be enshrined as one of the immortals of the game, for there was nothing that he could not do well on the gridiron. He was fast and elusive as a broken-field runner and he had terrific power through the line. He was one of the hardest men to bring down that ever carried a football. In more than 40 college games he never needed a time out. He often punted 70 and 80 yards and could place-kick up to 50 yards. Jim played 60-minute football, of course, and was in every play on defense and offense. He was a devastating tackler and blocker, a fine passer and pass receiver.

In 1911 when the Indians played Harvard, Jim, although bandaged heavily with two swollen ankles, shattered the Crimson line, ran wild around the ends, and kicked four field goals to beat a good team almost single-handedly, 18-15, and wreck an undefeated season for Harvard.

Later, Haughton said, "Watching him turn the ends, slash off tackle, kick and pass and tackle, I realized that here was the theoretical super-player in flesh and blood."

Jim made Camp's third All-America team in 1908. The following spring he left Carlisle and stayed out two years. The loose rules of the Indian trade school permitted the "students" to come and go almost as they pleased. Some stayed at the school for several years; others, homesick for the reservation, would return to it and after a year or two would come back to Carlisle. Jim drifted south and played semi-professional baseball for two summers in North Carolina. He probably would never have returned to Carlisle if Pop had not gone after him and persuaded him to come back to school. The coach told Jim that he had a good chance of making the United States Olympic team in 1912. In the fall of 1911 the big Indian came back to Carlisle. He was then 23 years old and 15 pounds heavier than he was when he played on the 1908 team.

Perhaps the finest and most complete tribute paid to the black-haired, good-natured Indian came from Grantland Rice. "All the wild laurels you can gather for the pick of the past in football belong to Jim Thorpe," he wrote in 1936. "The answer is simple — Thorpe could do more things well, even up to the point of brilliance, than any other player in the game."

One who agreed with those words all his life was Dwight D. Eisenhower, a first-string halfback on the Army team when Jim played against him at West Point.

Camp selected Jim on his first All-America teams in 1911 and 1912. Shortly after the 1912 season ended a Boston newspaper revealed that Jim had accepted money for playing baseball while he was away from Carlisle and was, therefore, a professional athlete and not entitled to his Olympic awards.

Jim admitted that the charges were true but said that he did not realize that he was doing anything wrong. Nevertheless, he was forced to return his Olympic medals and trophies, and his achievements at Stockholm were removed from the records. Sadly, he left Carlisle and spent the next several years playing professional baseball and football.

Pop Warner moved on to Pittsburg in 1915, lured by an offer of $4,500. In his first season there Pop's Panthers were undefeated, winning all eight games and rolling up 247 points to 19. In all his years at Carlisle, Pop had never had a perfect season. "The Indians had a tendency to become overconfident after they beat a couple of first-rate teams," he said. "They'd loaf and drop a game to a team that had no business beating them."

The Panthers did no loafing under Pop. They had perfect seasons in 1915, '16, '17 and '18 — shortened to four games because of World War I. Those were Pop's golden years of coaching.

The Carlisle Indian School closed its doors in August, 1918, to make way for wounded veterans of the war. It is now the Army War College. There is a bronze tablet near the old school that pays tribute to the great Indian athlete who once roamed its playing fields.

JIM THORPE

Olympic champion (2 gold medals), 1912. *Right:* Major league baseball player, 1919.

All-America college football player, 1912. *Right:* Professional football star, 1920's.

CHAPTER 7

The Golden Age and
the Glamor Boys

AMERICA'S GOLDEN AGE OF SPORT dawned in the wake
of World War I to produce the greatest array of colorful talent ever
gathered together up to this time. Eager to forget the holocaust of
war, the public seized upon sports with a fanatic zeal.

By 1920 the rush was gathering momentum and it accelerated
rapidly. The boom in sports stars was on. The names of Babe Ruth,
Jack Dempsey, Bill Tilden, Bobby Jones and Earl Sande rolled off
the presses from one newspaper edition to the next.

Football was now a national game. New and exciting teams
such as Notre Dame and tiny Centre College began to share the
limelight with the top eastern powers. George Gipp (The Gipper)
led Notre Dame to an unbeaten season in 1920 and also placed
on Walter Camp's All-America that year. In 1921 Alvin (Bo)
McMillin sparked Centre to a 6-0 defeat of Harvard in one of football's biggest upsets.

Two of the greatest names of all were those of Red Grange, the
famous redhead from Illinois, and the Four Horsemen of Notre
Dame. There were others, too, such as little Albie Booth of Yale;

Chris Cagle of Army; Friedman and Oosterbaan from Michigan, and Ken Strong, the New York University back — all of whom flourished during the 1920's. Chick Harley of Ohio State, who spanned World War I as an All-American in 1916-17 and again in 1919, also was a part of the era.

One of the questions posed in the midtwenties was never answered and never will be: what would have happened if Red Grange of Illinois had faced the Four Horsemen of Notre Dame? Although they were contemporary they never met on the playing field and gray-haired fans still speculate upon the probable result. Such a contest also would have pitted against each other two of the wiliest and wittiest coaches of all time — German-born Bob Zuppke of Illinois and Knute Kenneth Rockne, a native of Voss, Norway.

Harold Edward (Red) Grange, a modest youth from Wheaton, Illinois, the son of a deputy sheriff, became the greatest individual football hero of his day, and perhaps the greatest running back of all time at the University of Illinois. His speed and fantastic running

Bo McMillan

ability produced a legend all its own. He was called a "streak of fire, a breath of flame" by Grantland Rice, while Zuppke compared him to a "deer running freely on the plain."

Imaginative writers loved to dream up nicknames for him. Red became known as "The Galloping Ghost" and "Old 77" by reason of his jersey number, as well as "The Wheaton Iceman" because he delivered ice during summer vacations in his home town. Incidentally, he slipped under a wagon wheel and his left leg was so badly crushed that for a time amputation was considered.

Grange weighed only 125 pounds as a high school freshman and his father encouraged him in football by offering him 25 cents for every touchdown he scored. But after the first year he needed no incentive. He made six touchdowns in one game and kicked 30 consecutive extra points during the season.

By the time he reached Illinois he stood 5 feet, 10 inches tall and weighed about 170 pounds. He was so modest, however, that he tried to quit the frosh squad after he saw some of the talent around him. This included Earl Britton, who later became his blocking back, and Ralph (Moon) Baker, who transferred to Northwestern to become an All-America fullback. Fraternity brothers prevailed on him to remain on the squad, however, and then one day Zuppke watched him run back a kick 65 yards through the entire varsity, and the die was cast.

The Galloping Ghost made his debut against Nebraska on October 6, 1923. His famous orange number 77, flashed across the goal line three times in 39 minutes as Illinois won 24-7. Then Zuppke removed him from the worried gaze of opposing scouts. That the Nebraska Cornhuskers were no ordinary opponent was proved when they handed Notre Dame and the Four Horsemen their only defeat of the season. Grange went on to lead Illinois to eight straight victories without defeat, and he was the sensation of the year.

On October 19, 1924, Illinois dedicated its new Stadium at Champaign, and Grange appeared in the first of his two greatest games. He faced Michigan, a team without defeat since 1921 and ranked as one of the strongest defensive outfits in the country. Although Fielding Yost had retired temporarily as coach upon his

Red Grange, The Galloping Ghost of Illinois.

doctor's orders, the Wolverines, under Coach George Little, appeared as strong as ever. Yost was seated in the stands with Mrs. Yost, and he repeated an earlier prediction about Grange for the press.

"Meechegan won't give him room to run, ye knaow," Yost said in his West Virginia drawl. "Wherever he goes, he'll find eleven tacklers to greet him. Meechegan has faced great runners before."

But Michigan had never faced a runner like Grange, as Yost and 67,000 spectators soon found out.

The fleet redhead stunned the Wolverines and the record crowd on the opening kickoff as he dashed 95 yards to score. The next three times he handled the ball he raced for touchdowns again — on runs of 67, 56, and 44 yards. Four touchdowns within 12 minutes against what was called one of the nation's best defensive teams!

As Grange scored his second touchdown, Yost flung his hat away and dashed down from the stands, ignoring the pleas of his wife and his physician. He raged along the sidelines imploring his beloved "Meechegan" to hold, and to rally, but to little avail. The Wolverines did manage to score twice after Grange had been taken out, but the redhead returned in the final quarter to score again and pitch the touchdown pass that made the final score 39 to 14.

Once they recovered from the shock of seeing their champions humbled, Wolverine followers were generally high in their praise of Grange. One die-hard exception was a reporter on the student newspaper, *The Michigan Daily* who wrote, "All Red Grange can do is run!"

The words were not lost on Zuppke. Quick as a flash he countered with a quip that became a part of gridiron lore. "Yes," he said with his sly grin, "and all Galli-Curci can do is sing!"

Michigan, however, did gain some small measure of revenge on the same gridiron in 1925. Yost was back with one of his greatest teams, which had Benny Friedman and Bennie Oosterbaan as its stars. The field was muddy and Friedman contributed the only score on a field goal for a 3-0 victory. Grange gained less than 20 yards.

The East, the real cradle of college football had never seen the Galloping Ghost in action, and skeptics found it hard to believe the glowing prose they read. Grange might run wild on the midwestern prairie, but he had never faced a strong eastern team, and there were plenty of them around. Take unbeaten Pennsylvania, for example.

Red quickly convinced them — on a rainy afternoon in Philadelphia on historic Franklin Field. The date was October 31, 1925 — Halloween — and the Quakers must have felt they were victims of some ghostly prank.

Before the game the critics scoffed. Hadn't Michigan held the redhead to less than 20 yards the week before? Beat Pennsylvania — what a laugh! Penn had the national championship all but sewed up!

Then Grange took over. On the first scrimmage play he broke through tackle, pivoted away from a linebacker and beat his interference to the goal. Later he added two more touchdowns, his cleats kicking up little spurts of water as he dashed through the rain. Britton scored another counter, as Grange deposited the ball on the six-inch line for his teammate to take over, a gesture characteristic of him. The final score was 24 to 2 for Grange, as one writer put it.

Near the end of the second quarter when Penn was dazed and thoroughly beaten, Zuppke removed his star for a rest. As the weary, mud-splattered player walked to the sideline he removed his orange helmet and the crowd caught a glimpse of his auburn hair.

Suddenly a vast silence fell over the rainswept stadium and 63,000 spectators rose to their feet. Every man in the crowd removed his hat in one of the great dramatic moments of sports history. Again as he left the field near the end of the game, the crowd stood up once more. But this time the fans were no longer silent. A mighty cheer echoed far beyond Franklin Field. Red Grange had arrived in the East; he had convinced both the writers and the fans that he was the real thing.

Grange always gave generous praise to his prize blockers, Earl Britton and Wally McIlwain. He was delighted when Britton, in 1925, gained national recognition for his prowess. Although McIlwain and Britton cleared the way many times for the Ghost, the public scarcely knew their names.

In all, Grange lugged the ball 3,637 yards for 31 touchdowns in 20 games for Illinois, always against stacked defenses.

Much of Grange's success, aside from his natural attributes, was due to the sharp-minded little Zuppke, who changed his running style to the confusion of opposing defenses. Against Penn, for example, the Quaker scout report said he could run successfully only to his right, but he ran to the left instead to demoralize a fine team. Zuppke also used Grange to introduce his famous Flea Flicker, one of his many innovations. Briefly, it was a pass to an end, who in turn flipped it laterally to a halfback. He had others, too, always with colorful names — The Corkscrew, Sidewinder, Whoa Back, and Flying Trapeze among others. He gave them colorful names so that his players would remember them better, he said with a grin. He also is credited with inventing the huddle, and with using a psychologist to understand his players better.

Early in Grange's career, Zup taught him to run in an S-pattern by swinging wide, cutting back, and then reversing his direction again. It was an unnatural maneuver for The Galloping Ghost that took many hours of patient practice to perfect, but it paid off. An artist himself, both as a coach and a painter in oils whose pictures still hang in galleries, Robert Carl Zuppke handled Grange with consummate skill and understanding. Together they were unbeatable.

Grange made Walter Camp's All-America in 1923 and 1924. After Camp died in 1925, both Grantland Rice and the Associated Press placed Grange in the '25 backfield.

When he turned professional with the Chicago Bears after his final season, Grange was criticized in some quarters for doing what is expected of any college star today. He was reported to have split two million dollars with his business manager, C. C. (Cash and Carry) Pyle, but he did not forget to repay his father for the money that had been borrowed to put him through school, and to his everlasting credit, Harold (Red) Grange remained the same modest, likeable person throughout his subsequent career both on and off the field.

It was Grantland Rice who gave the Four Horsemen their name. Writing in the *New York Herald-Tribune* of October 19, 1924, he produced a lead that became a football classic. It read:

Polo Grounds, New York, Oct. 19 — Outlined against a blue-gray October sky, the Four Horsemen rode again. In dramatic lore they are known as Famine, Pestilence, Destruction and Death. These are only aliases. Their real names are Stuhldreher, Miller, Crowley and Layden. They formed the crest of the South Bend cyclone before which another fighting Army football team was swept over the precipice at the Polo Grounds yesterday as 55,000 spectators peered down on the bewildering panorama spread on the green plain below. . . .

Deep in the second paragraph the dazzled reader found the score: Notre Dame 13, Army 7. No matter — it was in the headline, anyway, and a legend had been created.

The Four Horsemen averaged only 160 pounds but they struck with deadly speed. Their average for a one-hundred yard sprint was 10.4 seconds in football uniforms. Crowley, the left halfback was the heaviest at 164, while stubby little Stuhldreher at quarterback, weighed a mere 154 pounds. Miller at the other halfback and fullback Layden each weighed 162. They were lighter than most high school backfields today.

Although they were on the 1922 Irish squad, they did not begin to function as a unit until the Carnegie Tech game of 1923. By then Rockne found that they complemented each other perfectly. From a set modified T, the four backs hopped with military precision into the box formation a split second before the ball was snapped.

The defense had no time to "read" or analyze the play, or even see if the quarterback handled the ball first. The formation became widely imitated and so controversial that a one-second full stop rule was initiated by the Football Rules Committee in 1927. By then, however, the Four Horsemen had become history.

The Horsemen galloped behind "The Seven Mules," as hardy a forward wall as ever graced a gridiron. They were not large but they were quick, and they blocked with deadly precision. Adam Walsh at center was a tough and witty tiger, who once played an entire game with both hands broken, so the story goes. His sharp tongue helped keep the backs from becoming cocky as the adulation of the press and fans poured down on them.

117

Notre Dame's Four Horsemen — Miller, Layden, Crowley, Stuhldreher.

Rockne developed a secondary team called the "shock troops" to relieve his lighter, faster regulars from time to time. Once he sent the "shock troops" in to block for the Horsemen, but within minutes the famous foursome was in deep trouble as the defense hit them before they could start. Rockne quickly sent his regular forwards, headed by Adam Walsh, to the rescue.

Walsh ambled over to the sweating and bloodied backfield. "What's the matter, boys — run into a little trouble?" he asked mildly.

The Horsemen instantly got the point — it was the Seven Mules, the infantry of the line, that paved the way to touchdowns.

The Irish hit full stride to win nine games in 1923, losing only to Nebraska, 14-7, but in 1924 they reached their ultimate peak in speed, grace and power. They ripped through Army, blanked Princeton 12-0; rolled past Georgia Tech, Wisconsin — and this time Nebraska — along with Northwestern and Carnegie Tech. They climaxed their final season with Notre Dame's only appearance in the Rose Bowl on New Year's Day, 1925, against Stanford.

The game itself became a classic. It was supposed to pit the bull-like rushes of Ernie Nevers, the Indians' triple-threat fullback, against the speed and ability of the Horsemen. The blond and hulking Nevers played with both ankles tightly taped, but he tore the Irish line to shreds. He carried the ball 34 times, gained 114 yards, but never crossed the goal line. Once he was halted only inches from it, and many Stanford rooters thought he made it. But just as many Irish followers swore he did not, and the officials agreed with them.

Meanwhile the slat-like Elmer Layden stole the show. After Stanford seized a 3-0 lead, he put the Irish on the scoreboard with a three-yard touchdown plunge. Then he intercepted a Nevers' pass to return it 70 yards to score, and followed with another 35-yard interception to add to the Irish total.

Afterward there was a hot argument in the dressing room between a Coast newspaperman and Don Miller, who was backed by Crowley. The reporter insisted that Nevers had crossed the goal line. "I had my field glasses on the play from the pressbox," he insisted. "I know Nevers was across the line."

Knute Rockne of Notre Dame. *Right:* Ernie Nevers, Stanford (1923-25), was an indestructible fullback who was considered by many as the finest ever.

Just then a stubby little fellow stepped from the shower room, a towel draped around his middle. "And I say he didn't make it," said the newcomer firmly.

"Yeah? And where were you?" demanded the reporter.

"Sitting on his neck," replied Harry Stuhldreher.

Fielding Yost of Michigan always called his 1925-26 teams his greatest, and in '25 the critics ranked Michigan with Dartmouth as the two leading teams of the year. The Wolverines used the famed passing combination of Friedman to Oosterbaan to throw opposing defenses into a panic.

Friedman had squirmed on the bench as Grange ran wild against the Wolverines at Champaign, but now he blossomed out as a brainy quarterback and a deadly passer. Oosterbaan, a blond sophomore from Muskegon, Michigan, had been an All-American high school gridder and basketball player, and he could bring down any pass he could touch. Possessed of large and gifted hands, he could leap high, snare the ball with one hand and fight off defenders with the other.

Michigan swept through five games undefeated, including a shocking 54-0 victory over Navy, and now faced a good Northwestern team on Soldier Field in Chicago. Interest in the game was so high that 75,000 tickets had been sold. But on the morning of the game the weather man took a vital part in the proceedings.

It started to drizzle early in the morning. Before noon the rain had become a downpour mixed with sleet and the wind increased to a 55-mile an hour gale by kickoff time. Officials considered calling the whole thing off but when more than 40,000 fans braved the weather, there was nothing to do but play the game.

Northwestern recovered a Friedman fumble in the first quarter, and when two line plays failed, Leland (Tiny) Lewis promptly gave the Wildcats a 3-0 lead with a field goal. Late in the weird contest, Northwestern, in the teeth of the gale, smartly downed the ball behind their goal for a safety to win 3 to 2.

Soldier Field figured in the news again in 1926 when it became the scene of football's first 100,000 crowd (actually 111,000) as Army and Navy played a thrilling 21-21 tie. Tom Hamilton of Navy drop-kicked his third extra point to tie the score.

120

ne of football's most fa-
ous passing combinations,
nny Friedman and Bennie
osterbaan of Michigan.

In the East that same year, Brown University brought on its
famous Iron Men, who gave their Alma Mater its only undefeated
season as 11 starters played nearly three straight games without substitution. They scored victories over both Yale and Harvard.

Another powerful eastern team — the New York University
Violets — enjoyed great success in 1926-27-28. It was spearheaded
by Ken Strong, who led the nation in scoring with 160 points before
he moved on to greater honors in the pro ranks. He also might have
made the grade in major-league baseball except for a wrist injury
received while with the Detroit Tigers.

While Strong led the nation's scorers in 1928, a fellow who did
not score a point saw his name in headlines from coast to coast

121

after the 1929 Rose Bowl game. Roy Riegels, a fine California center, was the victim of football's most famous blunder in a game at Pasadena against Georgia Tech. He picked up a Tech fumble and whirled around to dash toward his own goal. Despite the frantic shouts of his mates, he continued in the wrong direction. Finally, he was tackled on the one-yard line by fullback Benny Lom of his own team. But as Lom tried to punt out of danger, the kick was blocked for a safety to give Georgia an 8 to 7 victory. Too late for poor Riegels, the Rules Committee passed a rule prohibiting an opponent from advancing a fumble that strikes the ground.

Bronko Nagurski was born of Ukranian parentage at Rainy River, Ontario in 1908, about the time Jim Thorpe began to distinguish himself at Carlisle in far-off Pennsylvania. While he was still a child, Nagurski's family moved to nearby International Falls, Minnesota, where his father opened a grocery store.

The youngster grew into a huge, powerful youth and played football at International Falls High School. Although he was its mainstay, his team was weak and failed to win a single game while he played. Consequently he attracted little attention when he entered the University of Minnesota in 1926. Loyal hometown alumni, however, had written to Dr. Clarence W. (Doc) Spears, the football coach, about him, and Spears, a former Dartmouth All-America guard and coach at West Virginia, was at least mildly interested.

His interest quickened when he first saw the hulking youth at the start of fall practice. Spears noticed that the young giant seemed nervous and ill at ease, and he decided to needle him to see if his spirit matched his magnificent physique. As he approached the shy youth, he thrust out his hand. "My name's Spears," he said. "What's yours?"

"Nagurski," replied the youth in a high-pitched voice that was later compared with Jack Dempsey's. "Bronko Nagurski."

"Bronko!" chided Spears. "What a strange name!"

Instantly Nagurski's eyes flashed. "Well, Clarence isn't such a hot name either."

Spears chuckled but he never forgot that introduction; this kid would do all right.

Nagurski soon proved more than "all right." He ripped up the varsity line as a frosh player and started at varsity end in 1927. But the Gophers needed tackles and that was where Spears placed him. He received his first real baptism of fire against Notre Dame.

Rockne's teams had beaten the Gophers twice in succession at Minneapolis, and this game was scheduled for old Cartier Field in South Bend, where the Irish had not been beaten or tied in 22 years. It looked like a sure-fire bet for the home team.

Although Spears had faith in his untried sophomore, he wanted further assurance. So he secretly instructed the veterans flanking Bronko on either side to keep him fired up with jeers and constant abuse. He already knew that an aroused Nagurski could wreck any line.

Notre Dame seized an early 7-0 lead on a Gopher fumble, but a few plays later an infuriated sophomore tackle flattened three Irish blockers and jarred the ball from the runner's arms. Agile as a huge cat, he pounced on the ball on the Notre Dame 15. On the next play Herb Joesting, pile-driving All-America fullback, faked a plunge and fired a touchdown pass instead and the score was tied 7-7. Led by Nagurski's inspired charge, the Gophers ripped Rockne's line to shreds and drove home for another touchdown. But the officials ruled the ball carrier had stepped out of bounds in the scoring run. Again led by the mighty Bronko, the Minnesota forwards held Notre Dame in check to mount one more drive, but the gun sounded to interrupt the march and the final score was 7-7. Even Rockne congratulated Nagurski on his play, and both Bronko and the game made the sports headlines. He maintained his spectacular pace during the rest of the season. Then, in 1928 with Joesting graduated, Spears moved him to fullback on offense, although he continued to play also as defensive tackle.

Again he was a sensation until he suffered the only real injury of his college career when Minnesota lost to tough Iowa, 7-6. The Bronk came out of a pile-up and found he could not bend over to assume his fullback stance. So he asked to play tackle both ways, and finished the game despite the excruciating pain. Later it was found that three ribs had been torn loose from his spine. But instead of ending his career, he continued to see limited service until the traditional game with Wisconsin that always closed the season.

Nagurski was determined to play, so finally a heavy harness

was devised to protect his back and ribs. He was injured again in the first quarter but, after a rest, insisted on returning to the field.

On the opening play of the second quarter Minnesota recovered a fumble on the Badger 18. Fred Hovde, quarterback, —now president of Purdue University— glanced at Bronko. "Think you can do it?" he asked.

"Try me," Nagurski replied through clenched teeth as he shifted to fullback. He plowed through for nine yards on the first play. Lugging the ball on five successive plays he crashed over for the lone and winning touchdown to knock the Badgers out of the Big Ten title. It was one of the most amazing displays of sheer courage and power ever seen on the gridiron.

Then came 1929, his greatest season. With Nagurski again playing two positions — most of the time at fullback, however — the Gophers lost only to Michigan, 7-6, and to Iowa again, 9-7. Despite the loss to the Hawkeyes in which he played 28 minutes at tackle, Nagurski switched to fullback and raced 45 yards for the lone Minnesota touchdown. With big Bronko in the line-up, the Gophers lost four games in two seasons (1928-29) by a total of five points.

While the *New York Sun* actually named him to two positions, Grantland Rice placed him at tackle on his All-America. When Rice was asked to compare him with two other greats, Jim Thorpe and Red Grange, Rice declared that he believed a team of eleven Nagurskis could have beaten a team of eleven Thorpes or Granges. Doc Spears, who played him at every position except center and quarterback, always maintained he could have been an All-American at any position he tried.

It did not take the Chicago Bears long to snap him up in 1930. Shrewd George Halas signed him for $5,000, the greatest bargain or steal of all time, depending upon how you look at it. He would have been in the million-dollar class today, and a bargain at that price.

Bronko Nagurski, Minnesota All-America tackle in 1929. He also dou at fullback, and later starred with the Chicago Bears.

One of the great games of the early part of the Golden Decade was Yale's victory over Harvard in 1923, when Tad Jones told his squad, "Gentlemen, you are about to play for Yale against Harvard. Never will you do anything so important!" The words have been often quoted, sometimes cynically, but the inspired Elis strode forth on a rainy afternoon to defeat the Crimson for the first time since 1916, by a score of 13 to 0. Raymond (Ducky) Pond, an aptly nicknamed Yale right halfback, scooped up a fumble in the second period to race 67 yards for the first touchdown Yale had scored in 16 years at Cambridge. After Captain Bill Mallory added two field goals, the Eli fans tore down the Crimson goal posts and carried them back to New Haven. The '23 team was one of Yale's finest and boasted two All-Americans in halfback Bill Mallory and Century Millstead at tackle.

Yale also figured in another classic during the latter part of the decade as a mite of a youth named Albie Booth, called "Little Boy Blue" out-dueled Chris Cagle and Army's giants to win an un-looked for 21-13 victory. The mighty sophomore midget — all 5-feet, 6-inches of him — hurled his 144 pounds across the Cadet goal line to overcome a 13-0 lead and score three touchdowns as his mother saw him in action for the first time.

Army scored twice in the second period upon runs by All-America Chris Cagle and driving Johnny Murrell, but the tiny blue-clad quarterback erased that lead as he ran rings around the Army defense. Coach Mal Stevens sent him trotting on the field after the second touchdown, and an inspired Yale team gathered around him to completely shed the sluggishness that had featured their earlier play. From that moment on, Booth's name became a part of Yale's gridiron tradition.

A highlight of the Army-Navy long series came in 1924 when Captain Edgar Garbisch kicked four field goals to give Army a 12-0 victory with President Calvin Coolidge among the 80,000 spectators who watched the game at Baltimore.

Another team that turned in some excellent performances during the twenties was Boston College under Frank Cavanaugh, the colorful "Iron Major" who was a law professor and a successful trial lawyer as well as a football coach. His teams were unbeaten in both 1920 and 1926.

Interesting things were happening as well in the Southwest Conference at the other corner of the gridiron map. Ray Morrison, a scholarly young mathematics professor, also coached football at Southern Methodist in Dallas, Texas. When the Vanderbilt grad found that his lightweight teams could not match brawny foes on the ground, Morrison fashioned a glittering "aerial circus" that soon left fans gasping.

Opponents scornfully dubbed it "basketball on the grass" but when they could not cope with the forwards, laterals and double-laterals, they adopted the same tactics. The result was a wide-open attack such as the Southwest had not seen since frontier days. The SMU Mustangs sprayed the air with flying footballs and raced through unbeaten seasons in 1923 and 1926.

It took Joel Hunt of Texas A. & M., perhaps the greatest back ever developed in the Southwest Conference up to that time, to defeat the rarin' Mustangs in 1927. Hunt scored 128 points during that season as he called signals, ran, passed, punted, kicked field goals and extra points. The A. & M. Aggies led by Hunt downed the SMU Mustangs in one of the wildest games of the season, 39-13.

The trend toward wide-open passing had begun a new era of college football.

CHAPTER 8

Passes, Power
and Depression

THE GOLDEN TWENTIES CRASHED to a halt in October, 1929 but the impact of economic disaster was not immediately felt by college football. Millions of fans still turned out each autumn Saturday to watch their favorite teams.

Without doubt, the golden era produced the game's greatest period of growth up to that time. Super-stars flashed across the grid-irons, and new stadiums sprang up like magic. High school participation increased steadily as the names of Red Grange and the Four Horsemen became household words. Everywhere youngsters dreamed of college careers.

While the established powers of the East, the Middle West and Far West still captured the sports headlines, teams in every section were coming on with a rush, and the demands for new, fresh talent grew steadily. Soon any high school youth who could lug or pass a football better than his mates, or throw a healthy block, became a prize. The recruiting of the past had been at random, or on an individual basis done usually by an interested alumnus. With the rapid growth of the game it became an organized venture — the great talent hunt was on.

128

The 1930's brought still another important change to college football — the expansion of the passing game. More talent and better coaching produced skilled passers and receivers to be honed into potential scoring weapons at college level.

In 1934 the NCAA Football Rules Committee recognized the new trend by making three important changes: (1) the circumference of the ball was reduced, making it easier to throw; (2) the 5-yard penalty for more than one incomplete pass in the same series of downs was eliminated; (3) an incomplete pass was permitted to be grounded in the end zone without loss of the ball, except on fourth down. Previously all passes incomplete in the end zone were considered touchbacks.

This shift of emphasis did not come overnight since there were too many great power teams still around. Jock Sutherland's Pittsburgh elevens, particularly those of 1932-37; Minnesota teams coached by Bernie Bierman (1933-36); General Bob Neyland's Tennessee Vols (1939-40), and Southern California under Howard Jones in the late 1920's, were outstanding examples of power running behind deadly blocking.

r. John B. (Jock) Suthernd of Pittsburgh, one of e great coaches of his day.

These teams rarely passed except to vary the running attack. Often their plays were not difficult to diagnose — the trick was to stop them. It was as if they cried, "Here we come — try and stop us!" The defense was swamped by the wave of deadly blocking ahead of the runner. All of these power elevens were characterized by strong, aggressive lines, both on attack and defense.

Rockne and Notre Dame still rode high as the new decade opened. The 1930 team was called the Irish master's greatest, and had an exciting and colorful season, but it proved to be his last. It swept through 10 games without defeat after being held 14-14 until the final three minutes of the opener against Southern Methodist.

At this point the Irish took time out, and Scrapiron Young, the fiery Notre Dame trainer, seized his trusty first aid kit to hurry out on the field. First, however, he turned to Rockne. "Any instructions to the boys, Coach?" he asked hurriedly.

"No — just tell 'em anything will work if the blocking is right," replied Rockne.

The players crowded around the trainer as he approached. "Any word?" asked quarterback Frank Carideo anxiously.

Young gulped. Then shocked at his own temerity, he burst out, "Yeah! Call fifty and block like hell!"

The play won the game 20-14, and the Irish were off and running.

Navy was defeated 26-2, Pittsburgh 35-19, Pennsylvania, 60-20, and Northwestern, 14-0. Army gave the Irish their closest call in Soldier Field in Chicago. The game was played in rain and snow before 110,000 fans, but Notre Dame managed to eke out a 7-6 decision.

Then came the season's final test, against Southern California, and they played without ineligible Joe Savoldi or his replacement, injured Moon Mullins. But the determined Irish were still rolling and they overwhelmed the Trojans, 27-0. Thus ended a triumphant but painful season for Knute Rockne. Suffering from phlebitis, he had to have his legs bandaged before every game.

The 43-year-old Irish coach was at the peak of his fame that winter. He was sought after for speeches, invited to join business ventures, quoted almost daily in the press. Then tragedy struck. He boarded a plane for an appearance in Los Angeles, and as he changed aircraft at Kansas City, a ticket mixup left him without a seat. But a fellow passenger who recognized the great coach, generously gave up his own space. The day was March 31, 1931, and a few hours after the take-off in bitterly cold weather, the plane crashed in a cornfield near Bazaar, Kansas, killing all on board. As the stunned public grieved, members of the 1930 team acted as pallbearers, and funeral services were broadcast around the world.

Hunk Anderson, one of Rockne's most faithful disciples, took charge in 1931, and for a while it looked as if the victory march would continue. Then Big Ten champion Northwestern held the Irish to a scoreless tie, although the undefeated string still held up.

This year Howard Jones brought his Southern California Trojans to South Bend for the season's finale. The Irish quickly proceeded to score twice with Marchie Schwartz and Steve Banas setting up a 14-0 lead.

But the Trojans did not quit. They had such players as Gus Shaver, Ernie Pinckert, Aaron Rosenberg, each of them All-American before his career ended, and this day they rose to the heights. Shaver led two tremendous last quarter scoring drives, going over both times himself. But guard Johnny Baker missed the first extra point try, and USC still trailed by a point, 14-13.

Only four minutes remained as the desperate Trojans mounted their final assault. Two long passes by the inspired Shaver, a couple of Irish penalties and a three-yard loss left the ball on the 15. With time running out, quarterback Orv Mohler quickly called upon Baker for a field goal, and this time the kick was good for three points and a 16-14 victory. The 25-game undefeated streak that Notre Dame had launched in 1929, was ended by the Trojans. The luck of the Irish had run out.

* * * *

There was lively action in the Big Ten, too, as Michigan, coached by former Wolverine All-American Harry Kipke, parlayed the "punt, pass and prayer" system into four straight Conference titles, won or shared. Kipke proved that a team without a strong running attack could still win, provided it had good passing and kicking. In quarterback Harry Newman, the Wolverines had both, plus a smart field general and a tricky runner. As a senior in 1932 he was Grantland Rice's top choice at quarterback.

131

Northwestern shared the Big Ten title with Michigan in 1930, and with the Wolverines and Purdue the next year. The Wildcats from Evanston, Ill., had everything but good luck in 1931. Early in the season they lost "Hard Luck Hank" Bruder, regarded as a sure-fire All-American at halfback. He came down with smallpox after an unprecedented series of injuries the year before. Again, however, the Wildcats were undefeated in regular season Big Ten play. But the Depression was on in 1931 and a series of charity games was scheduled across the country. The Wildcats lost to once-beaten Purdue, and since Michigan also lost one game, the title was shared by all three with identical 5-1-0 records.

* * * *

Speaking of hard luck, how about the 1932 Colgate team coached by Andy Kerr? His Red Raiders did not yield a single point, becoming known as the team that was "unbeaten, untied, unscored upon — and uninvited," as they were bypassed in favor of Pittsburgh for the Rose Bowl bid. All they did was to score nine straight victories and pile up 264 points against such teams at NYU, Penn State, Syracuse and Brown. But Colgate had the last bitter chuckle: USC slaughtered the Pittsburgh Panthers, 35-0.

Kerr was one of the nation's most outstanding coaches for 18 years at Colgate, not to mention service at Pittsburgh, Stanford and Washington and Jefferson. He was more than a fine football tactician; he was a man of real stature.

Andy taught his players that enjoying the game was as important as winning, and he won plenty with his laterals, double spinners and other ball-handling magic. His first six Colgate teams lost but five games and in 1932 he gave his eleven the name of Red Raiders by ordering brilliant red uniforms for them.

Andy was one coach who refused to send instructions in to his players during a contest. "Why should I send in plays — let the quarterback call the signals," he once said. "If a coach wants to play so much — let him put on a suit and get in there himself!"

Kerr never missed a day's practice in 18 seasons at Colgate, and in the off-season he set a record of 29 years of coaching service with the East-West Shrine game in San Francisco, where his efforts helped raise more than 2 million dollars for crippled children.

* * * *

Andy Kerr, Colgate coach, who taught his players they could win and still enjoy the game. *Right:* Bernie Bierman guided Minnesota to six national championships.

In 1932 Bernie Bierman came North from Tulane to his Alma Mater, Minnesota, to succeed Fritz Crisler, about to begin his tenure at Princeton. By 1933, Bierman's young Gophers defeated a nifty Pittsburgh team, 7-3, and then played a scoreless tie with Big Ten champion Michigan, to demonstrate that they were real comers.

The following season the quiet-spoken, gray-thatched coach and his charges fired a bombshell into the national gridiron picture. Bierman came up with three massive, alternating lines and a bevy of hard-charging backs headed by halfback Francis (Pug) Lund and Stan Kostka, a 230-pound fullback, who could run hard and far.

Both Pittsburgh and Minnesota ranked high on the national scene in 1934, and their mid-October meeting practically decided top honors right there. This was the year the Rules Committee de-

Jay Berwanger, Chicago back (1933-35), was All-America in 1935 and the first Heisman Trophy winner.

creased the circumference of the ball by one inch to promote more passing, but for a time neither team seemed to have heard of the aerial weapon as they battered each other on the ground. In the final analysis, however, a lateral and a forward pass accounted for two of the three touchdowns scored.

Pitt counted first on a 67-yard run by halfback Nicksick, who took a lateral from fullback Izzy Weinstock and raced to the goal line. Minnesota's Kostka bulled over in the third period to tie it at 7-all. With 11 minutes gone in the fourth quarter, it was still even and the Gophers reached the Pittsburgh 23 on fourth down and four yards to go. As the defense massed to stop him, Kostka handed the ball backward to his quarterback, who in turn flipped it back to Pug Lund. Faking a run, Lund whirled and hurled a long diagonal scoring pass to his left end a couple of yards from the goal to give Minnesota a 13-7 victory. From 1934 through 1941, Bierman's teams won six conference and four national crowns.

On the 1936 team there was a tall, handsome quarterback, who had been an all-conference guard before Bernie Bierman made him into a signal caller. He earned letters in hockey and golf as well and was awarded the Big Ten Medal, given the senior at each school with the best record in both scholarship and athletics. His name was Charles (Bud) Wilkinson, and he passed up his father's bond business to become one of football's "winningest" coaches at Oklahoma a dozen years later.

* * * *

Jay Berwanger of the University of Chicago was the greatest individual rusher of his time from 1933 through 1935. A unanimous All-American halfback choice, he was the first winner of the John W. Heisman Trophy, and the first collegian ever drafted by the NFL, although he did not choose to play as a pro. Nicknamed the "Flying Dutchman" because of his speed and ancestry, and called the "Man in the Iron Mask" by reason of the leather-covered steel mask he wore to protect an oft-broken nose, Berwanger scored 22 touchdowns and kicked 20 extra points, playing on weak Chicago teams. He punted, passed, kicked off, played safety, and missed only one game in three years.

* * * *

Starting with an excellent sophomore class in 1933, Fritz Crisler developed three of the East's greatest teams at Princeton. His young Tigers were unbeaten in 1933, allowing only eight points to be scored against them as they shut out their first seven opponents. Included was Columbia by a 20-0 margin, the team that went on to the Rose Bowl to defeat Stanford in the 1934 classic.

Yale's light-hearted Larry Kelley caught the winning pass to upset the Tigers 7-0 in 1934 for their only loss. The game was all the more remarkable because Yale used only 11 men — marking the first time the Elis had gone the route without substitution in 37 years.

Crisler's legion had a close call in 1935, winning a 7-6 decision over Pennsylvania. From there on they simply riddled the opposition by scoring 256 points to 32 for the opposition. No eleven scored more than a single touchdown against the '35 team.

Larry Kelley, All-American Yale end, was one of the finest receivers of the mid-1930's. *Right:* Clint Frank, Yale quarterback, guided the Elis to an upset victory over Princeton in 1936.

Quarterback Cliff Montgomery dashes 25 yards as Columbia defeats Stanford in the 1934 Rose Bowl game.

It must certainly rank as one of the greatest Princeton teams of all time, and on a par with any of the elevens of its era.

Kelley, however, returned to torment Crisler and his Princetonians in 1936. Collaborating with Clint Frank, Yale's All-American quarterback, he engineered a wild upset to win 26-23. This was the same season that Kelley kicked a loose ball and recovered it himself to defeat Navy — and incidentally caused a rule change in 1937 to outlaw kicking a free ball.

Columbia drew undeserved ridicule when Stanford invited them to play in the 1934 Rose Bowl game. Despite the upset by Princeton, the Columbia Lions were a spirited, well-drilled team with an excellent record behind them. The adverse criticism only strengthened their determination to win.

Coach Lou Little, one of football's shrewdest minds, took full advantage of the situation. He quietly drilled his team in a special scoring maneuver — the now famous KF-79 — in which quarterback Cliff Montgomery and Al Barabas, a fleet halfback, were the key actors. They spent long hours perfecting their roles.

The game was played in a drizzle upon a water-soaked field. The huge and mighty Stanford Indians led by halfback Bobby Grayson, Monk Moscrip and other All-Americans, pushed their lighter opponents around with ease in the first quarter but did not score. Then, in the second period, Tony Matal, Columbia end, carried a pass to the Stanford 17.

Montgomery, the opportunist, now struck swiftly with KF-79. Earlier the play had failed to score, but now it worked to perfection. The quarterback took the center's pass, spun around and deftly slipped the ball to Barabas, faked a hand-off to the other halfback, and pretended to keep the leather himself. The defense chased Montgomery while Barabas raced around left end to cross the goal line untouched. The Lions successfully protected their 7-0 lead until the final gun.

The pressbox was loaded with red-faced experts. Among the major critics only Damon Runyon had picked Columbia — to needle a fellow writer, it was said. One rueful reporter with a sense of humor, led off his story with a quotation from the Bible.

"Now Barabas was a robber," he wrote.

* * * *

Frank Thomas, a former Rockne quarterback, followed Wallace Wade at Alabama when the latter became coach at Duke in 1931. Despite the change, the Alabamans kept right on winning and in 1934, a 9-0 record put them in the Rose Bowl on January 1, 1935.

Stanford started with a rush. After an Alabama fumble had been recovered by the Indians, Bobby Grayson quickly drove in to score. The extra point put the Coast team ahead 7-0. But as against Columbia the year before, the Stanford team was crossed up. Expecting a typical Thomas running attack, the Indians were hit with an aerial blitz in the second quarter that scored 22 points on three touchdowns, a field goal and one extra point. The outcome was settled in the first 12 minutes of that period.

Dixie Howell and Don Hutson each scored twice in the game. Howell counted the first touchdown after passes to Hutson and Bear Bryant put the ball on the five-yard stripe. A few minutes later Dixie flew 67 yards to count, and Alabama was rolling. Hut-

Don Hutson, Alabama end, 1932-1934, was one of the greatest pass receivers of all time.

son, the skinny kid who once trapped rattlesnakes as a hobby near his Pine Bluff, Arkansas, home, now snared flying footballs with the same intense concentration. Don had entered Alabama as a baseball player but he left it as an All-America end. He already had demonstrated the pass-catching wizardry that later made him an all-time pro wingman with the Green Bay Packers. In the Rose Bowl game he scored on passes of 67 and 54 yards. The final tally was Alabama 29; Stanford 13.

*　*　*　*

The Southwest Conference had its first national radio hookup by NBC in 1935. Billed as the "Game of the Week," it turned out to be a hair-raising contest. Southern Methodist was now coached by Matty Bell, while Texas Christian, the other principal, was guided by TCU's one-time water boy, Dutch Myers. Dutch had served TCU in that capacity as a youngster.

The SMU Mustangs had a great runner in Bobby Wilson, but TCU had Sammy Baugh, destined to become one of the greatest passers and punters of all time when he hit his real stride with the Washington Redskins.

Texas Christian's jittery receivers dropped nine of Baugh's

Sammy Baugh, great passer at Texas Christian, later became an all-time pro star with the Washington Redskins.

bullet passes while the SMU Mustangs seized an early 14-0 lead. But Sammy finally hit one to make it 14-7 at the half. The score remained that way until the fourth quarter when Baugh pitched another strike to make it 14-all.

Then on fourth down, SMU faked a punt. Kicker Bob Finley swung his leg, then stepped back and hurled a long high pass to Wilson, who made a fantastic leaping catch to give Southern Methodist a 20-14 victory. The win made Southern Methodist the league's first Rose Bowl representative.

Lest defense football be forgotten in the rush of passes and powerhouse tactics, how about Fordham's Rams, and their "Seven Blocks of Granite?" In 1936 this great line held all opponents to a single touchdown. Unfortunately that led to the season's only loss, 7-6 to New York University. For three seasons the Rams played scoreless ties with Pittsburgh, and in 1937 allowed only 16 points to be counted against them.

The "Blocks" whose names were as tough to pronounce as their line was to penetrate, were a nightmare for writers and announcers. They included Alex Wojciechowicz, Berezney, Babartsky and Jacunski, among others. Less difficult was that of Vince Lombardi of the 1936 team, who became famous as coach of the Green Bay Packers and the Washington Redskins. This rugged Fordham gang was coached by Jimmy Crowley, who had been a member of Notre Dame's Four Horsemen. From 1933 through 1941, the Rams were a real power in the East.

The Ohio State-Notre Dame game played at Columbus, November 2, 1935, certainly ranks with the greatest contests in college football's first century. For sheer thrills, excitement and drama, it is hard to find its equal.

Ohio State's steam roller was guided by Francis A. Schmidt, who brought the "razzle-dazzle" North with him from Texas Christian, where he had coached for several years. His unbeaten Ohio Buckeyes had lost only one game in 12 starts — to Illinois in 1934 — and they featured a spectacular attack that mixed power with flashy laterals. Schmidt was a showman who loved to run up big scores. Notre Dame, had won from Kansas, Carnegie Tech, Wisconsin, Pittsburgh and Navy in its first five games by substantial, but not overwhelming margins in 1935.

The 81,108 fans lucky enough to get tickets to the contest leaned forward expectantly as the game got underway. They were waiting for Schmidt to unleash his combination of power and dipsy-do, and he did not disappoint them. Ohio State wheeled up and down the field for a 13-0 half-time lead. Both touchdowns were spectacular. Fullback Frank Antenucci intercepted a pass, then flipped a lateral to Frank Boucher as he was about to be tackled. Boucher raced 73 yards to score. The second touchdown came after a 50-yard drive that featured a double-lateral pass play.

Irish coach Elmer Layden started his second team in the third quarter. Only Bill Shakespeare's fine kicking kept the Buckeyes in check. But Andy Pilney, at safety, returned a punt to the Ohio 12, just as the period ended. Two plays later Notre Dame had its first touchdown on a pass by Pilney, and a one-yard plunge by fullback Steve Miller. The extra point was missed and the Irish still trailed 13-6.

A few minutes later, however, Notre Dame recovered a Buckeye fumble and marched 78 yards to score. Pilney began to pass. He hit Wally Fromhart on the 33. Then he fired to Mike Layden, brother of Coach Elmer Layden, in the end zone. But again the conversion point failed, and it looked as if the Irish luck had run out. There were less than two minutes left, and Ohio State still clung to the lead, 13-12.

What followed was worthy of a script by Bill Shakespeare's namesake. The Buckeyes fumbled once more, this time at midfield. Unbelievably, the Irish recovered the ball for another chance. Pilney dropped back quickly, found all his receivers covered, and took off on a twisting dash of 32 yards before he was knocked out of bounds on the 19. But his knee was injured on the play and he had to be carried from the field.

Shakespeare hurried in, missed with his first pass, and with 32 seconds left, shot a second to Wayne Millner behind the goal line to win the game, 18-13.

In connection with the observation of football's first one hundred years, a panel of veteran writers was asked by the NCAA to pick the most outstanding game of the century. Although they were not all in agreement, one choice did emerge, by a substantial margin — the Ohio State-Notre Dame game of November 2, 1935.

The Buckeyes figured in a similar thriller against Cornell in

Bill Shakespeare of Notre Dame punts against Ohio State in 1935.

1939. Once more Ohio State seized a two-touchdown advantage. Then Pop Scholl scored for Cornell on a 79-yard dash, and passed for another TD — only to leave the Buckeyes ahead, 14-13, when the extra point was missed.

Again Ohio State rooters looked for a tremendous second-half surge. But it was Carl Snavely's Cornell team that put on the drive to win 23 to 14, and continue on through an unbeaten season.

After its perfect 1939 record, Cornell came up with another powerhouse in 1940. Ohio State was repulsed for a second straight year, and the Big Red steamed forward confidently until the Dartmouth game. Then came one of the most famous incidents in gridiron history.

Dartmouth surprised everyone by seizing a 3-0 lead, and still held it with four and a half minutes left. Cornell had the ball on its own 48, when little Pop Scholl went on a passing rampage to move the Big Red to the Dartmouth 5. Three line smashes reached the one-

Bob Kreiger of Dartmouth kicks the field goal that won the famous "Fifth Down" game with Cornell.

foot line with only seconds left. Cornell tried to call time out and drew a five-yard penalty. Scholl's desperate fourth-down pass was knocked down in the end zone, and Dartmouth rooters went wild, believing their team had won, 3-0.

But suddenly Referee Red Friesell signaled that Cornell had another down. The surprised Dartmouth team protested but Friesell merely placed the ball back on the 6-yard stripe once more. The Big Red eleven huddled quickly, thinking a double offside had been called, which nullified the play. This time Scholl's pass to Russ Murphy in the end zone was good and when the extra point was kicked, Cornell apparently had won, 7-3.

But afterward Coach Carl Snavely was puzzled. He studied the game film carefully and realized his team had been *given* a fifth down by mistake. So Cornell authorities quickly sent a wire to Dartmouth relinquishing their victory and extending congratulations to Dartmouth, the winner, 3-0. The famous "fifth down" became history.

The game was a bitter disappointment to the Big Red team, since it had lost its chance for the national title to Texas A & M., led by "Jarrin" John Kimbrough, one of the greatest fullbacks the Southwest ever produced.

There were many stars during the 1930's, but a few deserve special mention. Byron (Whizzer) White of the University of Colorado, led the nation in rushing and scoring in 1937. Whizzer, an All-America back, was a Phi Beta Kappa, and a Rhodes Scholar. He served in the Navy in World War II, and went on to climax a brilliant law career by becoming a justice in the U.S. Supreme Court.

Another Phi Beta Kappa was Nile Kinnick, Iowa's All-America quarterback, who also appeared to be destined for great things. However, his career was cut short when he died as his Navy fighter plane crashed in the Pacific during World War II.

Three fine black athletes also were among the standouts of the decade. They were Brud Holland of Cornell, twice an All-

Brud Holland, the Cornell All-America end, later became U.S. ambassador to Sweden. *Right:* Jackie Robinson, UCLA halfback, was the first black athlete to play major league baseball.

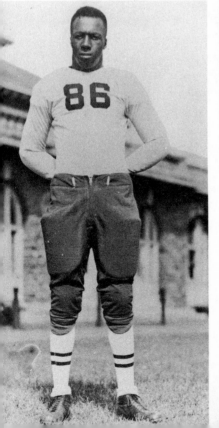

America end, and UCLA stars Kenny Washington and Jackie Robinson. Washington became a top professional gridder while Robinson was the first of his race to play major league baseball when Branch Rickey signed him with the Brooklyn Dodgers. In 1970 Dr. Jerome H. (Brud) Holland, president of Hampton Institute in Virginia was appointed Ambassador to Sweden by President Nixon. These three joined such famous predecessors as Fritz Pollard of Brown; Paul Robeson, Rutgers end, who became world-famous as an opera singer, and Duke Slater, great Iowa tackle, later a judge in Chicago.

The decade had its disappointments as well. The University of Chicago dropped football in 1939, and Stanford failed to win a single Pacific Coast Conference victory. Amos Alonzo Stagg, whose name always will be synonymous with Chicago, was spared this final blow, since he had been coaching for seven years at the College of the Pacific. Clark Shaughnessy, who had succeeded Stagg now also left for the Pacific Coast — for Palo Alto and Stanford. His brief case bulged with a new offense — the T-formation with a man in motion — the modern T which he had learned from George Halas and Ralph Jones of the Chicago Bears while serving as their part-time assistant. The formation was destined to revolutionize college football.

CHAPTER 9

The New T and the Touchdown Twins

THE 1941 STANFORD-NEBRASKA Rose Bowl game made the collegiate football world conscious of the modern T-formation.

Perhaps no other single contest had so great an impact upon the college sport since Knute Rockne and Gus Dorais of Notre Dame unleashed their pass attack upon unsuspecting Army for a 35-13 upset victory in 1913. On New Year's Day, 1941, the T-formation with a man in motion, which the Chicago Bears already had exploited so well, become a formidable weapon in the college field.

Coach Clark Shaughnessy, however, was greeted with derision when he announced in Palo Alto in 1940 that he would teach the T. There were immediate repercussions from the fans, alumni and even the players. What was this T stuff, they wanted to know? Didn't this mossbacked guy from has-been Chicago know this was 1940, not 1900?

But the somber-faced Shaughnessy calmly went about the business of teaching the tricky T, with a man in motion, that he had learned with the Chicago Bears' coaching staff.

"The first time he diagrammed a play on the blackboard, I didn't know whether to laugh or walk out," said Frankie Albert, who had been a so-so halfback on the 1939 team. "Whoever heard of a back charging into a line without a blocker ahead of him? It looked like suicide!"

Within a few short months, however, Stanford's comeback brought out the fans to watch this magic ball-handling team march through an undefeated season that included a victory over Southern Cal, 21-7. Although the AP poll named Minnesota as No. 1, the Helms Foundation chose Stanford.

How had Shaughnessy done it? After studying movies of the previous season, he converted Albert, a left-handing passer, to a T quarterback. Albert became fascinated with the new role. He did not run or block. Shaughnessy wanted him clear-headed to call plays, pass, or feed the ball to the other backs. They would then explode their T magic through brush-blocked linemen, or scamper around baffled ends. The new coach taught that it was not necessary to flatten the opposition, when a check or nudge would brush them aside long enough for the speedy back to race by.

Fast-starting little Pete Kmetovic was placed at left half, with swift Hugh Gallarneau on the right, and Norm Standlee, a bull-dozer of a man, at fullback. This was the nucleus of the "Cinderella Team" that raced through nine victories and into the Rose Bowl.

There was the usual widespread clamor over choosing the other sectional representative. Many wanted Minnesota, but when Nebraska was selected the fans were satisfied. The Cornhuskers had lost only to the Minnesota Gophers, and they were a tough and respected team.

As the game opened, it looked as if another dream was about to be blasted as Nebraska marched 79 yards to score in the first two minutes and seize a 7-0 lead. Then Frankie Albert unleashed the T. Kmetovic skipped 29 yards, then knifed through to the 11, and Gallarneau scored. Albert kicked the first of three successful conversion points to tie it up.

Nebraska recovered a Stanford fumble and drove in to score again, but the extra point was missed. The Indians countered with a 40-yard pass play, Albert to Gallarneau, and Stanford led at the half, 14-13. In the third quarter came the celebrated "perfect play."

148

Stanford prepares its new T magic for Nebraska in the 1941 Rose Bowl game. The backs are Gallarneau, Standlee, Albert and Kmetovic.

Clark Shaughnessy, Stanford coach, brought the modern T to college football in 1940.

Kmetovic caught a punt on his own 39, and his teammates blocked out every Nebraska player as little Pete scored without a hand being laid upon him. The count was 21-13 for the Indians, and that was the final result as well.

The game became a classic; every coach in the land wanted to know how it happened. The T itself was nothing new, and neither was the man in motion. But never had the two been forged into such a weapon as Stanford had thrown at a fine Nebraska team.

The coaches did not know the whole story. Shaughnessy, an ex-Minnesota tackle and fullback under Dr. Williams, came from Tulane and Loyola of the South to succeed Stagg at Chicago in 1933. He became interested in watching the Chicago Bears on Sunday, particularly their use of the T. By chance he met Ralph Jones, the man who brought this new version of the formation to the Bears. Together with George Halas they studied a weakness in it. They found it had real striking strength up the middle, but as Halas later recalled in *The Chicago Bears*, an interesting book by Howard Roberts: "We had no way of getting around the ends effectively until Clark and I figured out 21 different ways to skirt them. Our T's biggest fault became its greatest asset."

The result of the 1941 New Year's Day game almost caused a stampede toward the new formation, epecially when Frank Leahy junked the Notre Dame box and shift in 1942, his second year as Irish coach.

Many of the older and highly successful coaches stuck to their own offenses, although some incorporated certain features of the T that might fit into their own style of play.

One such coach was Don Faurot at Missouri. He had lost his ace triple-threat back, Paul Christman, by graduation. Christman, since widely known as a TV sportscaster, could run, pass or punt, and with no successor coming up, Faurot was ripe for a change. The Missouri coach quickly modified the new system to his needs to finish fifth nationally in rushing and gain a bid to the Sugar Bowl with rather ordinary players. Then when World War II came along, he took his formation with him to the Iowa Pre-Flight School where he was sent by the Navy to coach football and help condition future fliers.

Faurot's new attack was known as the split-T, in which the quarterback became a runner as well as a passer, thus differing from

Shaughnessy's T at Stanford. He spread his line wide and the quarterback ran laterally behind it, ready to run or throw. This became the "option," or "keeper" play as we know it now. While in the Navy, Faurot met Bud Wilkinson and Jim Tatum, both of whom liked the split-T and went on to make it famous.

Lou Little combined the blocking technique of the standard single-wing formation with the T's deception to develop what became the winged-T. From it he evolved an optional pass or end run play that enabled Gene Rossides, star Columbia back, to throw touchdown passes on the first play against Rutgers and Dartmouth in 1946. Rossides' pass to Bill Swiacki in 1947 ended Army's 32-game undefeated streak 21-20.

Later Davey Nelson, Delaware coach, became highly successful with the winged-T. During five years, three of Nelson's teams won the Middle Atlantic Conference title and the Lambert Trophy.

151

Working with a former Michigan teammate, Forest Evashevski, coach at Iowa, Nelson refined and perfected the formation. Evashevski's Hawkeyes won two Big Ten and two Rose Bowl championships with it in 1956 and 1958.

*   *   *   *

During his career at Michigan in 1938-39-40, Tom Harmon was perhaps the most colorful and exciting player to watch since Red Grange. Gifted with the same kind of explosive speed as the Illinois redhead, Harmon scored three touchdowns against Ohio State in his final game. This brought his TD total to 33, or two more than Grange recorded in three less games.

The handsome, rugged 195-pound Gary, Indiana, athlete was more versatile than Grange. Tom kicked extra points and field goals to bring his scoring total to 237 points, and he threw 16 touchdown passes. He also was an outstanding punter and a fine defensive player. His last two years he was a unanimous choice for All-American, and he was the Heisman winner as a senior.

Michigan's Tom Harmon gets a new jersey after ripping through opposing tacklers.

Tom won 14 letters in high school in four sports after almost getting kicked off the grid squad as a 14-year-old freshman for popping his bubble gum while the coach was talking. As punishment he was sent in to return punts against the first stringers, and when he returned one 95 yards for a touchdown, the bubble gum was forgotten.

Harmon's confidence in himself was superb; he was at his best when the chips were down. Once Bennie Oosterbaan, then assistant coach in charge of Michigan's pass defense, warned big Tom about a particularly dangerous pass receiver on the opposing team — an All-American wingman that Harmon was supposed to cover.

After the coach had emphasized the seriousness of the situation, Harmon smiled and said, "Don't worry about a thing, Coach. I'll bet you a double malted he doesn't catch a single pass."

Oosterbaan stared at the halfback in amazement, then accepted the bet. Next day he watched Harmon snatch the ball in front of the famous end and return it for a Wolverine touchdown. The opposing end spent a miserable afternoon; it was the only time in his career that he failed to catch at least one pass.

Harmon collected his malted, and Oosterbaan's favorite saying, even today is: "Don't worry about a thing, Coach."

Tom really hit his stride in 1939 as the Wolverines defeated Yale and Pennsylvania but lost to Illinois and Minnesota in the Big Ten. He engaged in a sensational scoring duel with Francis Reagan, great Penn back, in a game finally won by Michigan 19-17. Against Iowa, Harmon scored all of his team's 27 points, as the Wolverines won.

One of his greatest performances came against California in 1940. The date was Tom's twenty-first birthday and he observed it in spectacular fashion. He ran the opening kickoff back 94 yards for a touchdown behind perfect blocking. Later he sprinted 72, 86 and 8 yards to count again, and then fired a scoring pass for good measure as Michigan won 41-0.

* * * *

Pearl Harbor signaled the entry of the United States into World War II, December 7, 1941. Gas rationing and travel restrictions caused the transfer of a number of games and resulted in a sharp drop in attendance. The '42 Rose Bowl game was switched from Pasadena to Durham, North Carolina, where Wallace Wade's Duke team was beaten by Oregon State, 20-16. The Army-Navy game was played in Annapolis for the first time since 1893, with 12,000 fans attending instead of the usual 100,000 in Philadelphia. The picture looked bleak for both professional baseball and college football until President Roosevelt decided that both sports were needed to help boost home morale.

Football's value as a conditioner was recognized and the sport sprang up in many service training centers. A Navy program that permitted college trainees to engage in varsity sports helped no end. Commander Tom Hamilton, the man behind the naval aviation cadets' physical fitness program, emphasized strongly the importance of wartime football.

Soon his Navy pre-flight schools which conditioned young men for the rigors of flying, had such coaches as Bernie Bierman, Don Faurot, Harvey Harmon and Jim Crowley to help toughen the Cadets. Army camps also were fielding teams to stimulate their fitness programs. In the colleges the rule barring freshmen competition was rescinded for the duration as college men entered the services in ever increasing numbers. Perhaps the best of all service teams was that of the Great Lakes Naval Training Station, the same center that produced the top service eleven of World War I.

* * * *

In the East, Denny Myers had succeeded Leahy at Boston College, and his 1942 team looked even greater than the 1940 team. It rolled up 261 points to 74, and led the nation in weekly press association polls as it took the field against the Holy Cross Crusaders, four times beaten and once tied.

Then disaster struck. The lowly Crusaders came to life to blast the Eagles 55 to 12, in a stunning upset. But the defeat turned out to be the luckiest break the Boston College players would ever have. They had made reservations at the Coconut Grove club in Boston for a victory dinner. Naturally, they cancelled them. That evening a flash fire swept the club to claim 492 lives in one of the worst holocausts in the nation's history.

* * * *

154

Nineteen hundred and forty-two proved to be a year of upsets, and among the victims was Georgia Tech's Ramblin' Wrecks, one of the strong teams of the South. Ranked No. 2 behind Boston College in the early season polls, they were smacked down by Georgia. The Georgia Bulldogs were led by an awkward but powerful back named Frankie Sinkwich, and he was aided by Charley Trippi, a sparkling sophomore. Sinkwich had been an All-American the year before, and he led the country in both rushing and passing, despite a broken jaw which caused him to wear a protective steel brace. The Georgia eleven, coached by Wally Butts, swept on to its first Southeastern title, but Ohio State, under the tutelage of an ex-high-school coach, Paul Brown, won the AP poll. Brown entered the service shortly after and Carroll Widdoes filled in for him in 1944.

The Holy Cross Crusaders scored one of football's biggest upsets by downing Boston College 55-12 in 1942. John Grigas, Crusader fullback, plunges for a gain.

Widdoes had a great quarterback in Les Horvath, Heisman winner that year, who piloted Ohio State to the Big Ten title.

When Brown returned to take over again, his teams won several championships, both national and conference before he joined the Cleveland Browns professional team to go on to further honors.

* * * *

Although the civilian schools still trying to play football suffered heavily, the service academies, Army and Navy, never had it better. They produced some of the greatest teams in their long history.

Coach Earl (Red) Blaik had come to West Point from Dartmouth a couple of years before, and by 1944 he was ready to unleash one of the most devastating attacks in football history upon Army opponents.

Blaik had a marvelous one-two punch in Felix (Doc) Blanchard, a swift and bruising 205-pound fullback, and Glenn Davis, lightning fast and shifty at 175 pounds. They soon became known as the "Touchdown Twins," and by reason of their running techniques, as "Mr. Inside," and "Mr. Outside." Burley Doc Blanchard would blast between the tackles, and then turn on his speed to reach the goal line. Davis raced wide around the ends, and then cut back with a deceptive change of pace. Together the Touchdown Twins were almost unbeatable. If the defense spread wide, Blanchard would go rampaging through the middle. When it closed in, Davis would have a field day of his own. To aid them on their touchdown forays, and also to put up a stout defense, Army had Doug Kenna, Arnold Tucker, Barney Poole and big Tex Coulter, to name a few of the other Army stars.

The Twins, both All-America choices three years running, led Army to a record 27 victories, one tie and no defeats. In 1944 the Cadets gained at least partial revenge for 13 years of defeat by Notre Dame as they won 59-0, the worst defeat in Irish history. The following year Blanchard and Davis slacked off a bit but Army won again, this time 48-0. They also spearheaded the Cadets to three straight wins over Navy. From 1944 through 1946, they scored 89 touchdowns and counted 537 of the 1,179 points Army scored during that period.

Army coach, Earl (Red) Blaik, discusses tactics with his "Touchdown Twins", Doc Blanchard, left, and Glenn Davis.

An unexpected result of Army's awesome rise to power was the development of the platoon system in 1945. Michigan faced the prospect of meeting the Cadets in Yankee Stadium with a thin, wartime squad laced with 17-year-old freshmen, allowed to play under relaxed wartime rules.

Wolverine coach Fritz Crisler feared that his youngsters would be overwhelmed by the bigger, more mature Cadets. Then he smartly took advantage of a 1941 rules change that allowed practically unlimited substitution. No one had realized its significance until Crisler recalled it.

The Michigan coach divided his line into offensive and defensive groups to offset the cadet speed and power, alternating them as the ball changed hands.

157

Fritz Crisler at Michigan invented the two-platoon system in 1945.

"We arrived at the two-platoon system not out of any great ingenuity on my part but because of pure necessity," Crisler said later. "Rockne used a somewhat similar system with his shock troops in the 1920's, but not quite the same way. It would be pleasant to say we defeated a vastly superior Army team with it, but we didn't. However, we did manage to hold them 7-7 for almost three quarters before Blanchard and Davis shook loose to win 28-7."

The Michigan coach next extended the system to the backfield, and soon complete units were trotting on and off the field regularly. West Point's Blaik, too, was impressed. In 1948 when the rules allowed the referee to call time out whenever the ball changed hands, Army also adopted platoons, and the idea spread rapidly.

Army's Black Knights still galloped in 1946, with a mark of 25 straight victories. But now the war was over and Notre Dame was undefeated, too. The meeting between the two teams was flamboyantly advertised as the "Game of the Decade," and it ended in a scoreless tie. Once Johnny Lujack brought down Blanchard in

Glenn Davis dashes 15 yards for Army against Notre Dame in the score-less tie of 1926.

an open field to avert a certain touchdown; in turn, Arnold Tucker saved a Notre Dame TD in a similar situation. The Black Knights rolled on without defeat until 1947 when Columbia shocked them and the entire football world with a 21-20 victory to break a 32-game undefeated string.

* * * *

Michigan had a super-team of its own by 1947. Led by backs Bob Chappuis and Bump Elliott, the swift Wolverine platoons raced to an unbeaten season, climaxing it with a 49-0 Rose Bowl victory over Southern California.

The score, the same by which Fielding Yost's Michigan team defeated Stanford in the first Roses game of 1902, prompted an inebriated fan to shout in disgust, "Forty-nine to nothing again! They haven't improved a darn bit in 46 years!"

The All-America Wistert brothers starred at Michigan. *L to R:* Alvin, 1948-49; Albert, 1942; Francis, 1933.

Former All-America end Bennie Oosterbaan succeeded Crisler in 1948, as Michigan won the AP poll with an unbeaten record. The Wolverines were led by tackle Alvin Wistert, the third brother in the same family to become an All-American at the same position.

The Wistert brothers are an interesting story themselves. The sons of a Chicago detective slain while thwarting a holdup when they were youngsters, the boys were raised by their mother, and eventually helped each other through Michigan. Francis, the eldest, became an All-American in 1933, while Albert made it in 1942. Alvin, the third brother spent four years in the Marine Corps before entering college. He won his All-American status at the age of 29 in 1948 and 1949.

*   *   *   *

One of the greatest backs of the 1940's was Doak Walker of Southern Methodist. A few years ago Southwest Conference sportswriters chose him as the league's greatest player since World War II. A three-time All-America back and a Heisman winner, Doak edged out Bobby Layne, colorful Texas quarterback, for the honor. Later they became teammates on the Detroit Lions football team.

Walker stood 5 feet, 10 inches tall, and weighed 170 pounds. He was neither fast nor a particularly good passer. But as sportswriter Will Grimsley wrote in his book *Football — Greatest Moments in the Southwest Conference:* "Doak Walker had a faculty for producing the big play at the big moment." So it was ironic that perhaps his greatest game ended in a tie with Texas Christian in 1947.

The contest was a thriller from start to finish. Walker scored two touchdowns but SMU still trailed 19-13 as the clock ticked off the final moments. Then the Mustangs scored on a pass, and Bill Stern, broadcasting for NBC, became so excited that he shouted into his mike, "Southern Methodist Goes Ahead, 19 to 19!" to the confusion of millions of listeners.

Walker had kicked 18 extra points that season but now he was dazed and exhausted and the ball went wide. So the final score remained at 19-all.

Grimsley describes an amusing incident as the rival coaches, Dutch Meyers of TCU and the Mustangs' Matty Bell, shook hands after the game. Meyer said, "God was with Southern Methodist today, all right."

"What do you mean?" snapped Bell. "God *is* a Southern Methodist!"

CHAPTER 10

The Rise and Fall
of the Platoons —
The Fifties

PLATOONS, PLATOONS, and still more platoons!

By 1950, more than 75 percent of the major colleges had followed the lead of Michigan and Army, and platoons were shuttling on and off college gridirons with monotonous and confusing regularity as the ball changed hands. While coaches refined and perfected the regimentation of specialists, the vexed fans booed and hunted frantically through their programs in a vain attempt to keep up with the players on the field.

Then colleges began to realize they had a bull by the tail. Squad ranks had been swollen for a time by returning servicemen under the GI Bill. But mass substitution meant that teams had to be six-deep instead of three-deep, as they had been when the athletes played both ways. Recruiting expenses grew heavier, coaching staffs had to be increased to handle the unwieldy squads, and soon the strain of added expense had become a factor too heavy for many schools to bear.

The 1951 official NCAA Football Guide listed more than a score of schools that had dropped the sport. Among them were such teams as Georgetown, DuQuesne, Catholic University, City College of New York, St. Mary's College (California), Niagara College — all names that had long been familiar to sport page readers.

The Korean undeclared war and the uncertainties of the draft further complicated and increased the need for more football material.

As the problem grew, the Rules Committee dealt the platoons a knockout blow in 1953, despite the anguished protests of the coaches who had voted overwhelmingly to retain liberal substitution. But the committee was adamant, and the new rule read, "A player withdrawn from the game may not reenter the same period except during the final four minutes of the second and fourth periods." Ironically, the man who started the system, Fritz Crisler, was chairman of the committee that year. He went on to become the second lifetime member of the group, following the footsteps of his own mentor, Amos Alonzo Stagg, and he helped formulate much major legislation.

Agitation for the old rule's return began immediately, especially since the pros adopted the system with great success. But while the restriction was loosened gradually in the latter part of the decade, a long time passed before anything like the freedom of the 1940's and early fifties prevailed.

As the new decade began, however, some extremely interesting football was being played under the platoon system. In 1950 there were three major teams which had long undefeated records — Notre Dame, Army and Oklahoma. Yet by the time the season was completed, including the 1951 bowl games, all three had fallen.

The Irish with the longest streak — 39 games without loss — were the first to fall. Purdue handed them a 28-14 setback early on the schedule.

Army had begun another march after Columbia halted an unbeaten string in 1947. They amassed another undefeated string of 28 games by 1950, before they faced a Navy team that had a sad 2-6 record. But the Midshipmen slapped them down 14-2 in the greatest upset of the year.

Oklahoma, after losing its opener to Santa Clara in 1948, won 31 consecutive victories before facing Kentucky, coached by Bear Bryant and led by quarterback Babe Parilli, in the 1951

Bud Wilkinson was one of football's "winningest" coaches at Oklahoma from 1947 until 1963.

Sugar Bowl. The Kentucky Wildcats promptly shattered the string, 13-7, and Bud Wilkinson and his Sooners had to start all over once more.

Oklahoma's rise to national power actually began in 1946, when Jim Tatum became head coach, and brought his ex-Navy sidekick, Bud Wilkinson, along as his assistant.

Wilkinson became the Sooners head coach in 1947, when Tatum went to Maryland. Bud quickly marshaled his redshirted forces and began a history-making march of 17 years. Tatum led the Sooners to one conference title. Wilkinson added 14 more. Three of those seasons — 1950-55-56 — brought national crowns based upon the press association polls.

Wilkinson combined the precision blocking he had learned

from Bernie Bierman with the split-T tactics of Don Faurot. His Oklahoma teams were among the first to stress the T quarterback as the ball carrier in a strong ground attack. Jack Mitchell, the Sooner field general, became the Big Seven's leading rusher in 1947. During his three seasons he scored 17 touchdowns with the spinner play Wilkinson taught him. Taking the snap from center, Mitchell would whirl around, hiding the ball with his body, then fake, hand it to another back, or run with it himself.

One of Wilkinson's greatest coaching jobs was done in 1950 when he lost 18 of 25 top players by graduation. All of his starting team except fullback Leon Heath graduated, and yet he turned out a championship outfit. Perhaps one of his most satisfactory victories came in the 1954 Orange Bowl when the Sooners defeated Maryland and his old buddy, Jim Tatum, 7-0.

Wilkinson, like Andy Kerr, always had the love and respect of his players, and he was as much an influence on them off the field as on it. On road trips he always insisted that his players dress neatly. "You are representing your university," he would say with a smile. "You don't want those people to think we're a bunch of *Tobacco Roaders*, do you?"

Billy Vessels, an All-American halfback, once commented, "He can inspire you by talking quietly far more than the ranting, raving type."

While Vessels was one of Wilkinson's top stars, there were many others such as Darrell Royal, Jim Weatherall, Max Boydston, Jerry Tubbs and Tommy McDonald, to mention a few.

Wilkinson had his arguments with other coaches but he never held a grudge. In the Orange Bowl game of 1954, Jim Tatum raised a question about the legality of the Sooners blocking technique. Yet not a word of the argument ever reached the press, and the two coaches remained friends afterward. When Oklahoma lost in 1952, some newspapermen questioned the legality of Notre Dame's shift, claiming it was designed to draw the opponents offside. Wilkinson refused to discuss it and told his players to do the same.

After that loss, the Sooners rolled through 47 consecutive victories for an all-time major college record. In 1957 the Irish ended the streak again, 7-0.

It is possible at this point to detect a sudden gleam in the reader's eye. Yes, indeed, there have been longer *unbeaten* strings, but we said *winning* records.

Three teams have gone longer without a loss. Washington went 63 games without defeat from 1907 to 1917, but was tied four times. During 1901 to 1905, Michigan was undefeated in 56 starts, but was tied by Minnesota after 29 wins. And then there was California with 50 undefeated starts but four ties from 1920 to 1925.

When Wilkinson retired in 1964 to enter politics for a time, the personable Sooner coach had recorded 145 victories, 29 defeats and four ties over a 17-year span. He was succeeded by his former assistant Gomer Jones.

The Notre Dame team that broke the Sooners' long string in 1957 was coached by youthful Terry Brennan, who played for the Irish under Frank Leahy. When ill health forced Leahy's retirement in 1953, he left coaching with the best record of any of Rockne's former pupils, a mark of 107 games won, 13 lost and nine tied, including a 39-game unbeaten streak from 1946-50.

* * * *

Television began to give college football a new problem as the decade opened. Game attendance decreased, and the falling gate receipts were often blamed on the telecasts. It was established that in television-serviced areas in 1950, there was a 4.2 percentage drop from the 1947-48 average. So at its annual meeting the National Collegiate Athletic Association decided to place a one-year ban on live telecasts by a vote of 161-7. No sooner was the vote announced than political pressure was brought to bear. Bills were introduced in five states to force university authorities to televise their games. The regents and trustees of these schools scratched their heads thoughtfully; many of their institutions depended on state funds, and were subject to strong public pressure within their own areas.

For a time some conferences, the Big Ten, for example, experimented with various plans, including "delayed" telecasts in which complete films of games were shown, usually on Saturday night or Sunday. By 1955 the National Collegiate Athletic Association (NCAA), which represented most of the colleges and universities, came up with a plan to pool all football television rights of

166

member institutions and share television proceeds equally. Generally speaking, this plan is still in effect, although schools are limited in the number of times they may appear in a season, either in regional or national TV games. These restrictions may be lifted in the case of sell-out games or post-season bowl contests.

* * * *

Ohio State's final game of the 1950 season, on November 25, was one of the strangest in football annals. The team had topped the AP national poll in mid-November, only to lose to Illinois. But Ohio was still in the running, facing a decided underdog in injury-weakened Michigan. The Illini faced a much weaker opponent in Northwestern, and so confident were Illinois students and authorities that they purchased gold footballs, emblematic of victory, to give the team after the Rose Bowl game. Scouts were sent by both Ohio and Illinois to watch California in its final game with Stanford, but Michigan did not bother to waste money on such a long trip.

Then the weather man took a hand. A savage blizzard swept the Middle West, and by game time the temperature had dropped to ten above zero. Less than half of the 83,000 ticket purchasers for the Ohio-Michigan game were on hand for the kickoff, and the number dwindled steadily during the contest.

The snow was so blinding that frustrated Coast scouts on hand to watch the Buckeyes, scrawled such laconic reports as this: "Visibility from pressbox, zero. Temperature 10 above and falling — wind velocity, 35 miles per hour."

A former teammate handed Michigan center Carl Kreager a pair of new pigskin gloves just before the game. "Take 'em," he urged. "You can't pass the ball with frozen hands." Kreager accepted them and did not make a bad pass all afternoon.

Ohio State kicked off, but neither team could go anywhere. Deception and tricky ball-handling were impossible, and blocking was almost as bad. The game developed into a record-breaking session of 45 punts — 24 by Michigan's Chuck Ortmann and 21 by Vic Janowicz of Ohio State.

Then the Buckeyes got a break. They managed to reach the Wolverine 27, and Janowicz, peering through the blinding snow, booted a field goal to give Ohio a 3-0 lead. But shortly afterward, the Buckeyes tried to punt and the kick was blocked. It bounded back behind the end zone for an automatic safety to make the score 3-2.

Only 40 seconds before the half ended, Ohio had the ball back on its own four-yard line. Everybody expected the Buckeyes to try to stall out the clock but they punted on third down instead. Tony Momsen, Michigan linebacker, crashed through to block the kick and fall on the ball for a touchdown in the end zone. A moment later the score was 9-3 when the extra point try was good, and that was the score at the half — and at the end of the game.

Michigan gained only 27 yards all afternoon and failed to make a first down as they blocked kicks for their points. Ohio had only three first downs and Janowicz had the longest gain of the day, an 11-yard skid around end. Only three of the 18 forward passes thrown by both sides were completed — all by Ohio State — as passers simply could not find the shadowy receivers.

An endless wait followed in the icy pressbox until the results of the Illinois-Northwestern game came through. Northwestern upset the Illini, 14-7, and Michigan was the Big Ten title winner. The Wolverines went on to defeat California 14-6 in the Rose Bowl.

Those gold footballs Illinois had purchased for the team? They were sold to Michigan to be presented to the new champions.

* * * *

The Michigan State Spartans were voted into the Big Ten in 1949 to replace the University of Chicago. Because Conference football schedules already were drawn up through 1952, they had to wait until 1953 to play a full league card. The Spartans did not pine away during the interim, however, as Coach Clarence (Biggie) Munn led them through several successful seasons.

They had embarked on a 28-game winning streak that was not broken until Purdue upset them 6-0, in their first Big Ten season. The loss was their only one, however, and they ended in a tie with Illinois for the Conference title. Since they were the loop's newest member, and the Illini had played in the Rose Bowl before, the Michigan State team was chosen for the trip to Pasadena. There they defeated UCLA in a 28-20 thriller to make their first year in the Big Ten a huge success.

Munn packaged the T and the single wing into what the press termed a "Multiple offense," and he used it successfully through

Clarence (Biggie) Munn, was Michigan State's first Big Ten coach.

1954 when he gave up coaching to become Michigan State's athletic director. He left a winning record of 54-9-2 behind him.

Hugh (Duffy) Daugherty, whom Munn had brought with him from his previous post at Syracuse, moved up from line coach to head man. A stocky lineman with a ready wit, he had played for the Orange. A broken neck received in his junior year handicapped Duffy, yet he was back as captain, wearing a neck brace, his senior year. World War II service then claimed him, but he returned in time to join Munn as assistant at East Lansing.

Daugherty started slowly, but by 1955 his Spartans were second in the Big Ten. Ohio State won the title, but since they had been to the Rose Bowl the year before, the second place team was sent to Pasadena. The Spartans made an auspicious debut by defeating UCLA 17-14 in a game that was decided in the last seven seconds on Dave Kaiser's field goal. It was Kaiser's first attempt in a regular game.

Another team in the national spotlight during the early 1950's was Princeton, one of football's most revered names. Coached by Charley Caldwell, the Tigers had their first two perfect seasons in

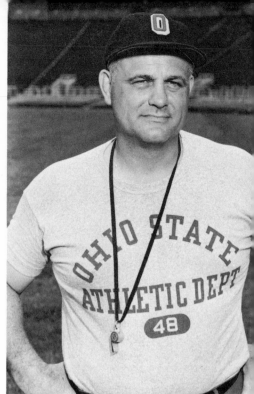

Dick Kazmaier, Princeton's all-around back. *Right:* Woody Hayes, long a successful coach at Ohio State.

the modern era. The winning streak was extended to 24 games in 1952 before it was snapped by Pennsylvania, 13-7. Twice Princeton won the Lambert Trophy and the eastern championship.

Caldwell had Dick Kazmaier as his ace, and Dick, who could run, pass or kick equally well, led the country in total offense with 1,827 yards rushing and passing as he took the Heisman Trophy in 1951. He was the first eastern player ever to win the national total offense title, and while he led in touchdown production with nine, he also passed for 13 other TD's.

Despite Princeton's excellent record, they rated no higher than sixth in the polls both years. Many critics felt that this was an injustice, and that the Tigers were far superior to some of the higher ranked outfits.

Certainly they were well-drilled by Caldwell, who won Coach-of-the-Year honors in 1950, and they had excellent spirit and personnel. Caldwell proved his right to rank along with his old coach, Bob Roper, and with Fritz Crisler, as one of Princeton's greatest mentors. The 1955 team also was a winner, with Royce Flippin in Kazmaier's tailback position.

Moving westward toward Ohio State, Woody Hayes had succeeded Fesler as Buckeye coach. He was a split-T man although he paid little attention to the forward pass. His teams rushed 89 times out of every 100 plays, the statistics showed in 1957.

Critics often scoffed at his driving offense through the years, saying that without passing it lacked imagination. One writer declared that it consisted of "three yards and a cloud of dust" as it chugged along, sparked by such backs as Howard (Hopalong) Cassady and Bob Ferguson during the 1950's. Although his ground attack produced a winning record, the controversial Woody sometimes threatened to modify it by putting in more passing, and to some extent he did. But when the chips were down, it was the fullback who got the call.

Out on the Pacific Coast still another team became prominent during this time. The University of California at Los Angeles, usually known as UCLA or the Bruins, rose up to challenge its powerful neighbor, Southern California. UCLA teams had rarely rated above average until Henry (Red) Sanders moved to the Coast from Vanderbilt to show the Bruins their proper place in the sun.

Sanders was a single-wing exponent, and enjoyed a reputation as a practical joker as well. He soon proved he was not joking on the field, however, as the Bruins trounced their cross-town rivals, the Trojans, 39-0. Before long, the new coach was winning popularity contests with the citizens of Los Angeles, and the student body as well.

Red Sanders proved his ability with a 42-11-1 record in six seasons. His undefeated 1954 team was named national champion by the UPI poll as it became the country's top scorer with 367 points against 40 for the opposition. The AP picked Ohio State, but the Bruins had a strong case.

Pacific Coast Conference football of the era was marred by dissension among the schools as charges of excessive recruiting and subsidization flew back and forth. It was a period of name-calling and bitter recrimination that was sad to see. All of this was aired in the press until college authorities and public alike were thoroughly disgusted. The mess ended in dissolution of the Conference. Southern California, California, Stanford, UCLA and Washington pulled out to form the Athletic Association of Western Universities that became known as the Big Five. It was later expanded to include Oregon, Oregon State and Washington State to form what is now known as the Pacific Eight Conference.

*   *   *   *

Another significant event took place in 1956. There were some good teams in the East such as Pitt, Penn State and Syracuse, as well as Princeton in the Ivy League. But the Ivy schools, the core of eastern football for so many years, had never gone along with the increased pressures of recruiting, and now they decided to de-emphasize the game. So in '56, they began playing in a formal, low-geared league. Spring practice was abolished, scholarships were presented on an academic basis, and players were barred from post-season all-star games. While this policy may have reduced some pressures, it did not produce topflight teams, nor did it attract the public. Pennsylvania, long a leader in attendance, saw historic Franklin Field drawing crowds of 20,000 in a 78,000 capacity arena.

Attendance began to rise again in the 1960's, bolstered largely by established traditional rivalries such as Yale-Harvard and Harvard-Princeton. Penn State and Syracuse continue to attract good followings, but generally crowds have been somewhat spotty. There is one contest, however, the annual Army-Navy game at Philadelphia, which still draws more than 100,000 spectators. It's the sentimental favorite of the American public.

*   *   *   *

Another team which attracted wide attention in 1958 was Louisiana State in the Southeastern Conference, which also came up with a successful gimmick. Picked ninth in a 12-team league by the critics, the LSU Tigers finished on top in both national polls as they won 10 straight games.

Coached by 34-year-old Paul Dietzel, Louisiana State had a hard-running halfback in Billy Cannon. On the surface, however, it appeared that he had little else. But Dietzel was an astute judge of talent, and he used it admirably. Dividing his squad into three

172

groups, he picked a starting eleven from among his best players, boys who could play on both offense and defense. The starters were named the "White" team because this was the color of their practice jerseys. A second gold-shirted team was primarily an offensive unit. It was first called the "Golds," but later this was shortened to the "Go" team.

Dietzel was stumped for a name for his red-shirted defensive group, who he felt would bear a heavy burden, and he wanted to keep their morale high. Glancing at a nationally-syndicated cartoon strip called "Terry and the Pirates" he came up with the perfect name.

That afternoon he called out to his defensive players. "You're the Chinese Bandits from now on. Go out and get 'em!"

The boys loved it, and so did the public. Each group caught the spirit of the thing, and they battled to outdo each other in every contest. Cannon became an All-American and Dietzel was named Coach-of-the-Year.

*   *   *   *

By 1959, Syracuse had focused national attention upon eastern football again. The Orange zipped through 10 games without a loss to dominate NCAA offensive and defensive statistics. Coach Ben Schwartzwalder's hard-hitting team started fast against Kansas

Coach Ben Swartzwalder and All-America Larry Csonka, sparked Syracuse in 1967.

and followed up with victories over Maryland, Navy, Holy Cross, West Virginia, Pitt and Penn State. Then they moved into the Cotton Bowl, led by brilliant sophomore Ernie Davis, to whip the Texas Longhorns, 23-14.

Davis' career ended in tragedy. After twice winning All-America honors in 1960-61, he was stricken with leukemia. He seemed to improve, then suddenly took a turn for the worse. He had signed with the Cleveland Browns and was very anxious to play. But it was not to be. Ernie Davis faced death with the same fortitude he had displayed on the gridiron, courageous to the end.

* * * *

As the decade of the fifties moved toward the 1960's, the T-formation had almost completely replaced the single-wing. A few teams like Tennessee stayed with it for a time, but there was a steady movement toward two facets of the T introduced to college football by Clark Shaughnessy — the split-T and the winged-T. The split version, begun by Don Faurot at Missouri, became widely used as Bud Wilkinson at Oklahoma, in particular, exploited it.

Quarterbacks passed the ball or kept it to skirt the ends, dart between widely spaced linemen, or pitch out to flying halfbacks. The winged-T which combined blocking features of the single-wing with the quick-hitting T, also was popular. It allowed plenty of latitude for both passing and running.

With such backs as Paul Hornung of Notre Dame, Jim Swink of TCU, Jack Scarbeth of Maryland, and others to execute the new formations, the crowds turned out in increasing numbers each fall Saturday afternoon.

A new development awaited the fans as well, and it provided a further opportunity to put the foot back into football as a dangerous scoring weapon. How well it succeeded was quickly demonstrated in the national statistics as the new decade began.

CHAPTER 11

The Scoring System Changes

THE NCAA FOOTBALL RULES COMMITTEE startled the gridiron world in 1958 by changing the scoring system for the first time in 46 years. Not since 1912, when the value of the touchdown was raised from five to six points, had an alteration been made.

Teams now were permitted to try for a one-point (by kicking) or a two-point (by running or passing) conversion after a touchdown. While the change seemed small, it started a merry battle among coaches for a time, at least. Darrell Royal of Texas, an outspoken critic of the option, nevertheless took advantage of it to defeat Bud Wilkinson and Oklahoma 15-14 during the '58 season.

Then, in 1959, the Committee acted again. This time it widened the distance between goal posts from 18 feet, 6 inches, to 23 feet, 4 inches, inside measurement. The compromise was a gesture toward those who sought to put the goal posts back on the goal line as in professional football. Another change provided for free substitution for one player of each team when the clock was stopped. This was amended in 1960 to permit one substitute to

175

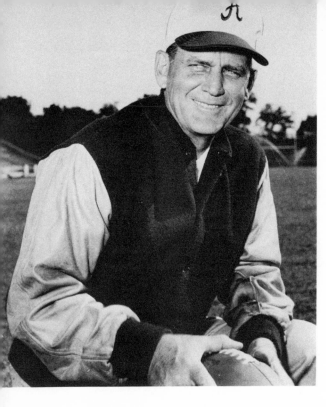

Paul (Bear) Bryant, veteran Alabama coach.

enter the game at any time between successive downs — the so-called "wild card" rule. These two changes resulted in a big increase in the field goal attempt, a tactic almost forgotten since the 1930's.

The increased popularity of the field goal as a weapon was reflected in the 1960 NCAA major college statistics. A record number of 224 field goals were kicked in major games — 25 more than were booted in 1959. Bill Dyas of Auburn kicked 13 three-pointers, four of which provided the winning margin for his team.

The toe was indeed back in football.

* * * *

Paul (Bear) Bryant, who returned to his Alma Mater — Alabama — in 1958, after being highly successful at Maryland, Kentucky and Texas A. & M., quickly got the Alabamans rolling again. By 1961 the team had hit the crest, scoring 11 straight victories, including a Sugar Bowl triumph over the Arkansas Razorbacks. The polls' choice and the Grantland Rice award all went to Alabama, and the Bear was named Coach-of-the-Year.

Incidentally, it might be in order here to interject a note upon how "the Bear" acquired his nickname. The story has it that Bryant, a native of Fordyce, Arkansas, once was persuaded by high school buddies to wrestle a trained bear when a traveling circus came to town. While the details of the match are vague, it is sufficient proof of Bryant's resourcefulness that he survived — but he became "Bear" from that time on.

He has developed 15 All-American players at Alabama, and including those selections at Kentucky and Texas A & M., he had a total of 24 in all. Among the more prominent are such Alabama stalwarts as Billy Neighbors at tackle; Dennis Homan, a fine end, and quarterbacks Joe Namath and Kenny Stabler.

Namath, the controversial $400,000 choice of the New York Jets pro team is perhaps his most widely-known player.

There are many stories about colorful, free-wheeling Joe, the kid from Beaverton, Pennsylvania high school. Some are good and others not so good. He was suspended for breaking training in his junior year, but he bounced back as a senior in 1964, determined to make up for his defection and prove just how good he could be.

Joe started with a rush. Against Georgia in the 1964 opener, he completed 16 of 21 passes, and scored three touchdowns to lead Alabama to a 31-3 victory.

With his publicity and his color, he was often the object of jibes from opposing players and the crowd, but he was undaunted. Once an opposing linebacker belted him unmercifully as he tried to pass, and jeered, "Hey you — No. 12 — down there on the ground! What did you say your name was?"

"Never mind — you'll see it in the headlines tomorrow, buddy!" replied Namath. He pitched a touchdown strike on the next play.

Because he carried the ball so much, Joe always wore special lightweight shoes made by a West German firm famous for its athletic footgear. Around them he wound heavy strips of white adhesive tape for added support. Another show-off gimmick — his detractors sneered. Against North Carolina State he was so irked that he did not tape them. Suddenly he was writhing on the ground with a twisted knee. Although he managed to play at least part of the remaining games, he was always in pain when he ran. But in the season's final game he completed six passes, one for a touchdown that gave Alabama a victory and an undefeated regular season.

It looked as if he might not be available for the Orange Bowl game with fifth-rated Texas when he was injured again in a light practice session. There was cartilage damage to the knee he had injured earlier against North Carolina State.

"I'll play," he insisted stubbornly, but no one expected him to make the grade.

Bryant kept him on the bench until Texas grabbed a 14-0 advantage in the second quarter. Then Joe stepped in to throw a scoring pass, and it was 14-7. But a penalty gave the Longhorns the ball, and they quickly scored again, making it 21-7.

In the second half Alabama staged a courageous comeback. Joe hit for six passes and 81 yards and the final toss was for a touchdown. Score: Texas 21, Alabama 14. Just before the third period ended, a field goal by Dave Ray narrowed the margin to 21-17. But Texas fought back, and it was not until the final moments of the game that Alabama moved down to the six-yard stripe. The clock was beginning to run out, and after three tries by fullback Steve Bowman, the ball was still a yard short of the goal line.

This was it — the whole game rested upon this play. Joe drove forward into the pile-up. One official started to raise his hand, but the referee shook his head, and Alabama had lost, 21-17.

As Joe limped toward the dressing room in despair, the crowd stood up to cheer his tremendous performance — 18 passes for 255 yards and two touchdowns. It was good enough to make Joe Namath the game's most valuable player. Ahead of him were the pros and a fabulous contract with the New York Jets.

*　　*　　*　　*

Oklahoma, a "down" team for two years, surprised everyone with its 1962 comeback. The Sooners were expected to rebound, but not for another season. Then Bud Wilkinson decided to gamble with a dozen inexperienced sophomores. After losing two of three non-conference games, however, it appeared that the coach's idea was a dud. Then the youngsters came to life and started ripping through the opposition. When the smoke of the battle had cleared, the youthful team handed Wilkinson his 14th league title in 16 seasons as chief of the Sooners. Courageous as those scrappy kids

Joe Namath, star Alabama passer, continued to win for New York Jets.

were, they could not hold off a veteran Alabama team in the Orange Bowl, and they lost 17-0. This was the personable Wilkinson's last title-winning season. He retired at its end at the age of 47, to enter public life.

* * * *

The Kansas Jayhawks, who finished fourth behind champion Oklahoma, Missouri and Nebraska in '62, had one of the country's best running backs in Gale Sayers, a six-foot, 196-pound young man who spent much of his boyhood on a farm near Speed, Kansas — perhaps a good omen for him because he certainly was endowed with rapid-fire legs.

Later Gale attended high school in Omaha, Nebraska where he starred in both football and track. Everyone assumed Sayers would enter Nebraska but he enrolled at Kansas instead. "Kansas was better in football at the time, and since I planned to play pro ball, I figured more pro scouts would see me there," the boy explained frankly.

Gale Sayers, swift Kansas back, became a star with the Chicago Bears.

Sayers, however, did not impress the scouts, who thought all he had was speed, even though he was an All-America back in 1963. But George Halas of the Chicago Bears saw film clips of the kid from Kansas, and snapped him up in the draft. Sayers quickly proved that the pro bird-dogs were wrong, by becoming one of the greatest running backs in the NFL. Halas paid Gale the supreme compliment by comparing him to George McAfee, Duke All-American in 1939, and one of the all-time great runners as a pro. Injuries had handicapped Gale both in college and with the Bears, but when he was right, they never came any better in Halas' book.

* * * *

Texas rode to the national title in 1963. The Longhorns became the first Southwest Conference outfit to win their league crown three years in a row. Coach Darrell Royal's boys won 10 straight games in 1963 and were invited to oppose Navy in the Cotton Bowl at Dallas on New Year's Day, 1964.

The game was a natural since Navy was ranked No. 2 in the polls on its 9-1 record, plus the fact that everybody's All-American, Roger Staubach, would pilot the Midshipmen. "Roger the Dodger" was already a legend in his time. A Heisman Trophy winner, he succeeded Joe Bellino, another great Navy back to that honor as one of Wayne Hardin's greatest protégés.

As a tremendous passer and a fantastic scrambler, Staubach had starred at Purcell high school in Cincinnati, O., before entering Annapolis, and he made good from the start. He led the nation's passers for two seasons, in 1962 and 1963.

Navy's only loss had come from Southern Methodist, also in Dallas, a 32-28 decision which had knocked them from the No. 1 spot, although they barely squeezed out a 21-15 victory over Army.

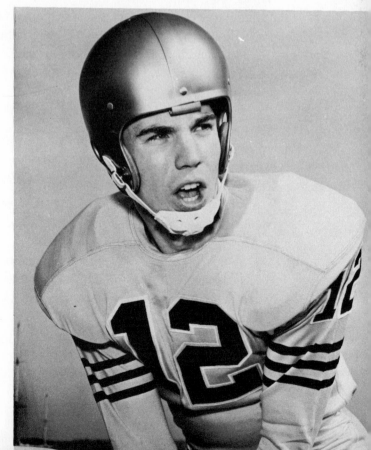

Roger Staubach, one of Navy's all-time greats.

A most unusual setting prevailed for the game. President John F. Kennedy had been assassinated in Dallas just six weeks before. There was great pressure both for and against the game from high sources.

Some thought it disrespectful for an Academy team to appear in the city where its commander-in-chief had been slain; others were equally adamant that the contest should be played as scheduled. These latter proponents felt that Kennedy, a Navy PT boat commander in World War II, and an ardent grid fan, would have wanted the game to go on. Protests from both sides poured into the Pentagon.

But Vice Admiral Charles Kilpatrick, Superintendent of the Naval Academy, declared firmly for the game, and Coach Wayne Hardin commented that it was in bad taste to associate the contest with the President's death.

On the eve of the struggle, anonymous crank calls were received by authorities threatening that the Cotton Bowl would be bombed if President Johnson's daughters, Lynda Bird and Lucy Baines, were present. They were guarded by Secret Service men as demolition experts searched the stadium for explosives up to game time. Hundreds of police guarded the stadium the night before.

Far from discouraging attendance, the threat of danger helped attract a sell-out crowd of 75,504, and wealthy Texas oilmen offered up to $200 a pair for tickets.

Meanwhile in other sections of the country, the polls were being ridiculed. The East, which had been exposed to Staubach, was especially critical, as most fans and writers proclaimed Navy the best team around. Some of the critics called the Longhorns a "cow country team" that did not belong in the same stadium with Navy. Such talk only fired up the furious Texans, almost as much as the Alamo had more than a century before. Coach Darrell Royal knew he had a red-hot team on his hands.

Staubach entered the game with a season completion mark of 107 passes on 161 attempts for 1,474 yards, and he had dodged and scrambled for another 418. He had had a hand directly or indirectly in 15 Navy touchdowns, and was a unanimous All-America choice as a junior. The great Navy athlete won both the

Heisman and Maxwell Trophies and the Walter Camp Memorial Award as well.

He did his best against Texas and was brilliant at times, but often he was smothered under an avalanche of orange jerseys, led by Scott Appleton, a 240-pound Longhorn tackle, who earned the "Lineman of the Day" award with 23 tackles.

Texas scored in the first three minutes. With the ball on the Longhorn 42, Duke Carlisle, slender Texas quarterback, shot a pass to wingback Phil Harris. The play was good for 58 yards and a touchdown, and the extra point gave Texas a 7-0 lead.

In the second period the Carlisle-Harris passing combo struck again for 63 yards to leave Navy behind 14-0. A Staubach fumble set up another Texas TD just before the half and it took the Longhorns only seven plays to score. Carlisle made the touchdown and the extra point brought it to 21-0. In the third period Texas drove to count again and make it 28-0.

Finally Navy got going to march 75 yards, and Staubach dove over from the 2. The Navy quarterback gambled on a two-point conversion that failed, and the final score was: Texas 28, Navy 6.

Staubach had done his best as he completed 21 of 31 passes for 228 yards, a Cotton Bowl record, but the Longhorns owned the game. In a fine display of sportsmanship, Vice Admiral Kirkpatrick entered the Texas dressing room and congratulated Coach Royal. "That was a beautiful game," he said. "There is no doubt about who is No. 1."

CHAPTER 12

The Platoons Return— More Touchdowns

PLATOONING RETURNED with a rush in the midsixties. In 1964 the rules were changed to permit unlimited substitution when the clock was stopped, and two men could be sent in while it was ticking. The rules became even more elastic in 1965. Now two players could be substituted at any time, and a full team was permitted to enter the game when the ball changed hands or when the clock was stopped.

Another change occurred in 1964 that had nothing to do with the rules, however, but it did help pep up the national scene. Notre Dame had not had a good team since 1955. Three coaches — youthful Terry Brennan, Joe Kuharich and Hugh DeVore — had produced only mediocre to average squads. In 1963 the Irish scored only two victories. That was too much; something had to be done, and something was.

Notre Dame authorities broke a long-standing tradition by going out of the University family to hire a new coach. He was a dynamic young man named Ara Parseghian, who had made a good showing at Northwestern despite the handicaps of meager material and many injuries. Parseghian had graduated from Miami University of Ohio where he played on the same team with Paul Dietzel.

184

Later as coach at Miami, from 1951 through 1955, his teams won 39 games, lost only six and tied one. Then he moved to Northwestern before going to South Bend.

Parseghian was a success from the instant he stepped on the Irish practice field. He put the platoon system into action in the spring practice of 1964. By fall he had two outfits ready to begin one of football's most sensational comebacks. The Irish swept through nine games without defeat, averaging 30 points per contest.

Week after week Notre Dame topped the polls. Quarterback John Huarte and Jack Snow, at end, combined in a forward passing battery that brought both men All-America honors, and Huarte the Heisman Trophy before he graduated. The Irish quarterback was equipped with a rifle arm while Snow had sticky fingers as well as speed afoot. They were a scoring threat every time they took the field.

Finally the Irish entered the stretch run for 1964 national honors. Only Southern California, the team that had upset their predecessors in 1931 and 1938 thrillers, barred the way to a perfect ten-game season. It was like the good old days, the fans exulted — the Irish versus Southern California, with all the chips down. It seemed unlikely that Notre Dame would fail this time.

Ara Parseghian brought Notre Dame out of the football doldrums.

Huarte and Snow helped Parseghian's athletes to a 17-0 half-time lead. But the Trojans lived up to their reputation as a comeback team. The USC forward wall caught fire in the second half to outplay the huge Irish line. Chunky little Mike Garrett, destined for All-American honors, led one scoring charge. However, Notre Dame bounced back to score again. Then a sharp-eyed official called a penalty against the Irish and the touchdown was nullified.

That proved to be the turning point. USC quarterback Craig Fertig sparked another scoring march and climaxed it by hurling a touchdown pass that cut the Notre Dame lead to four points — 17 to 13.

Then an Irish punt by Snow reached the Southern Cal 23. There, a holding penalty forced him to kick again. This time the Trojans got the ball at midfield, and their drive penetrated to the 15. Now it was fourth down with two minutes left in the game.

Fertig dropped back again, and brought the crowd of 83,000 to its feet by shooting a perfect pass to Rod Sherman to give Southern California a victory, 20-17. There was enough glory for both teams, however, in this dramatic finish.

Two-platoon squads were back and winging everywhere by 1965. There were other new and exciting developments as well, as coaches sought to outfox each other with trick formations and plays. Football language became a jargon to the bewildered layman.

Simple terms like "scrambling quarterbacks" and "sprintout passers" were relatively easy to understand. But what, the average fan wanted to know, was this "I-formation," or the "shotgun offense"?

Well, a scrambling quarterback was one who twisted and dodged behind his blockers, waiting for his receivers to break free, or if they could not, he might run with the ball himself, or keep it and take his lumps, hoping for better luck next time. The sprint-out guy headed out toward the sideline, then either passed, or turned upfield on a keeper play.

The I-formation, popularized among others, by Johnny McKay, coach at Southern California, in order to spring loose such backs as Mike Garrett or O. J. Simpson, was something else. The four backs lined up in a tandem behind the center at the start of the play. They might deploy as blockers for the ball-carrier, or shift wide for pass plays. The I had both power and deception.

Bubba Smith, giant Michigan State end, was a unanimous choice as All-American in 1966.

In the shotgun offense, the quarterback played about seven yards behind the line instead of up under center. The other backs would be spaced widely about two yards ahead of him. At the snapback, they would scatter like buckshot fired from a gun to receive a pass, or confuse the defense. Such formations all had one thing in common — they were designed to produce touchdowns in a variety of ways. Whatever the result, defensive coaches walked around, their eyes glazed, muttering irritably. And the fan who plunked his cash on the line for a ticket was also left slightly dazed.

Later the UCLA Bruins upset a hoary adage, usually applied to boxing, that a good big man can always defeat a good little man. The Bruins were a lighter, quicker, well-drilled team as they handed the Michigan State Spartans a stunning 14-12 upset in the 1966 Rose Bowl.

Michigan State's line was huge and it was not slow. Charles (Bubba) Smith, a 268-pound end, led an awesome five-man defen-

Gary Beban, UCLA, was one of the Pacific Coast's best.

sive line that averaged 244 pounds. Irrepressible coach Duffy Daugherty also had a barefooted Hawaiian kicker in Dick Kenny, about whom he quipped, "I make Dick trim his toenails regularly. Otherwise he ruins too many footballs."

Michigan State had topped seven Big Ten foes and won three games against outside competition, including Notre Dame, Penn State and UCLA itself, the latter by a 13-3 score in the season's opener. UCLA was 7-2-1 for the season to be a decided underdog. But what happened shocked both the experts and the fans.

Gary Beban, the excellent Bruin sophomore quarterback, was the key man in the upset, scoring a pair of quick touchdowns in the second quarter. A fumbled punt on their own six-yard line set up Michigan State for their opponents' first score. Beban scrambled to his left, cut back, and dashed across the goal line. Kurt Zimmerman's kick was good for the first of two all-important points.

UCLA then surprised the Spartans with a successful onside kick, to take the ball on the State 42. Five plays later Beban shot a pass to end Kurt Altenberg on the one-yard stripe, and then dove over himself for the touchdown. The conversion made the score 14-0.

But the Spartans fought back valiantly to score twice in the second half. Bob Apisa, at fullback, dashed 38 yards for one touchdown, and All-America quarterback Steve Juday scored another on a one-yard plunge. Both times, however, two-point conversion attempts failed, and UCLA won, 14-12.

Daugherty's earlier comment when a reporter asked him about his pet superstition— "It's bad luck to be behind at the end of the game" — was never more appropriate.

Alabama's lean, swift team was minus Joe Namath, who had graduated, but Steve Sloan was an excellent replacement. Sloan broke Joe's Orange Bowl passing record by completing 20 of 29 passes for 296 yards. Two of his tosses were for touchdowns, and he set up a field goal with another as Alabama defeated a much bigger and stronger Nebraska team 39-28. The loss spoiled Nebraska's first unbeaten, untied season in 50 years.

By defeating the third-ranked Huskers, Alabama jumped ahead of Michigan State in the final AP poll, although the UPI stuck with the Spartans. The Football Writers Association compromised by voting both teams a share in the top honors.

The year of 1965 also marked the passing of one of football's greatest figures. When Amos Alonzo Stagg died at the age of 102, it marked the end of an era. But perhaps this is not completely so since many of the formations and plays of today stem from his early genius and serve as a lasting memorial to him.

* * * *

Nineteen hundred and sixty-six was a banner year for the kicking game. Arnie Burdick of the Syracuse, N.Y. *Journal,* then president of the Football Writers Association of America, noted that 522 field goals were booted in '66, or five times as many as in 1958. One out of every nine games, according to Burdick's research figures, was won by a three-pointer, or 70 out of 626 contests were decided by the kicker's toe.

The player who really put the foot back in the game was Princeton's Hungarian-born Charley Gogolak, who escaped from his native land after the bloody revolution of 1956. Seven years later, in 1963, he became an American citizen and his Princeton teammates greeted him with a huge cake decorated with American flags at the start of fall practice.

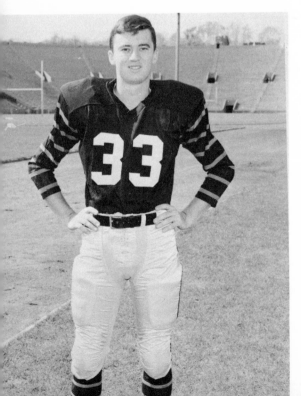

Princeton's Charley Gogolak
set six field goal records.

Gogolak's soccer-style boots set six American records. One of them that he broke — for consecutive extra points, — had previously been held by his brother Pete at Cornell. But records, like time and fame, are fleeting. As college football began its second century in 1969, only three of Gogolak's remained.

Jerry DePoyster of Wyoming, another phenomenal performer, completed three seasons in 1967 with a career total of 36 field goals and a high mark of 182 points. He also kicked three field goals of more than 50 yards against Utah in 1966 — boots of 54, 52 and 54 yards. His career total of six successful goals of more than 50 yards is the best ever in the first one hundred years of the game.

When he kicked his 28th field goal against Arizona to break Charley Gogolak's mark of 27, he said, "I was so happy I thought I'd pass out. You can't imagine the pressure. People even used to call me at 3 a.m. to offer advice."

* * * *

It was advertised as the "Game of the Decade" by the press, radio and TV — the 1966 meeting of Michigan State and Notre Dame. The contest was played in the Spartan stadium, and the NCAA released figures to show that 33 million television viewers watched it.

The State defense, led by Bubba Smith, George Webster, and their cohorts on the line, gave their South Bend rivals a rugged afternoon. But the Irish had some good defensive players of their own as well. Clint Jones led the Spartan attack on the ground, but the Irish had to play most of the time without the services of Nick Eddy and Terry Hanratty, both injured. While it was a hard-hitting game and great to watch, the result was a disappointing 10-10 tie that produced much argument. Spartan followers claimed the No. 1 spot, asserting that Coach Ara Parseghian had played for a tie rather than gamble to win in the waning moments of the game. The Irish fans believed he was right; it would have been foolish to take chances of a loss in their own territory.

One tangible result was that the roused Notre Dame squad simply slaughtered USC, 51-0, the next weekend to prove their title claim. State led the Big Ten for the second straight season but

Michigan State fullback, Regis Cavender (25),

was barred from the Rose Bowl trek since they had gone to Pasadena the previous year. So Purdue made its first Rose Bowl trip to win an exciting 14-13 victory when Southern Cal missed a two-point conversion with less than two minutes to go.

*   *   *   *

Eastern football enjoyed a fine season in 1966. Syracuse lost its first two games to Baylor and UCLA, and then won eight in a row and almost copped the Gator Bowl. The Orange won the Lambert Trophy as the best team in the East, sparked by the hard running of Floyd Little and Larry Csonka. They almost pulled out a victory in the Gator Bowl behind the dashes of Little, who set a new Bowl record by carrying the ball 29 times for 216 yards. But the Tennessee Vols battled hard, too, to win 18-12.

The big story of the eastern season, however, was Army's remarkable comeback. When Paul Dietzel left for South Carolina,

blasts the Notre Dame line in 10-10 tie, 1966.

Tom Cahill was suddenly made head coach. Cahill had coached the plebes (freshmen) for seven years, and he rose manfully to the new challenge. Using a lot of sophomores, making some offensive changes, he guided a losing team to the heights with an 8-2 record. The frosting on the cake was a 20-7 victory over arch rival Navy. Cahill also developed a fine young quarterback in Steven Lindell, and for a great over-all job he was chosen Coach-of-the-Year.

* * * *

While '67 was a wonderful year for spectators, it produced a bumper crop of frustrated coaches and critics.

The upsets came quickly. One of the most unusual happened on the national TV opener, September 16, when heavily-favored Texas A. & M. played host to Southern Methodist. The SMU Mustangs were three-touchdown underdogs but they refused to believe it. Seizing a 13-10 lead they clung to it stubbornly until the last 43 seconds. Then the favored Aggies forged ahead, 17-13.

A sub quarterback came off the Mustang bench after the next kickoff. He was Ines Perez, a tiny Mexican youth, barely 5 feet, 4 inches tall, who weighed 149 pounds. The crowd of 33,000 and the estimated television audience of 18 million could scarcely read his number (16) because it was partially concealed by his pants.

They were amazed when he began hurling passes with cool precision to his buddy Jerry Levias, a fine Negro halfback. Levias had played a magnificent game to help the Mustangs gain their early lead. He had run the last kickoff back 24 yards, and he was still glassy-eyed from the tackle as Perez began to throw. Afterward he could not remember those final seconds as he twisted and dodged to take Perez's passes to the A. & M. six-yard line with only four seconds left.

The tiny quarterback called a "curl-in" pass pattern and Levias sprinted for the end zone, cut in, and took a perfect pitch over his shoulder to make the final score: Southern Methodist 20, Texas A. & M. 17. Perez had taken his team 58 yards in the winning march.

Levias said later that he and Perez had worked out together all summer in Dallas. He estimated they had practiced the "curl-in" pattern "at least a thousand times." Perez added modestly that he "guessed they had been ready when it was needed."

The Texas Aggies appeared once more on TV, this time with a happier result. After losing four straight games, Coach Gene Stallings' boys roared back with six victories to win the Southwest Conference championship, and move into the Cotton Bowl against Alabama.

Stallings had played for Bear Bryant, now Alabama's coach, at Texas A. & M., and also had been Bear's assistant there. So it was inevitable that the old "pupil versus master" cliché would be revived, and the rivalry became even hotter.

In the Cotton Bowl Ken Stabler, who scored two Alabama touchdowns, counted his first early on an 80-yard march. But then one of his passes was intercepted, and Ed Hargett of the Texans, threw one in return, and the game was tied at 7-7. A 36-yard field goal put Bear's boys in front 10-7 before Hargett pitched another strike. Texas A. & M. led 13-10 at the halfway mark.

In the second half the Aggies marched 52 yards and made it

20-10 as Wendell Housley scored, and although Stabler counted belatedly for the Alabamans, the final score remained 20-16.

Despite his disappointment, Bryant hoisted his protégé high in the air in a mighty bear hug after the game. "The kid did a great job," he rumbled to the newsmen. "It was better coaching that did it."

Later, Aggie rooters shouted, "Stallings for President!"

"Nope," replied Stallings with a grin. "I like this job better."

* * * *

Southern California settled its well-publicized joust with Notre Dame early. The Irish were 12-point favorites at home but the redoubtable O.J. (Orange Juice) Simpson and his mates did not seem to mind. They rolled through to a 24-7 victory.

The 205-pound Simpson, with his sprinter's speed — he was a member of the USC world-record-smashing 440-yard relay team — led the Trojans to a 9-1 regular season record. The lone defeat came from Oregon State, 3-0, in rain and mud. Gary Beban and UCLA gave their rivals a scare until O.J. cut loose with a 64-yard scoring run to produce a 21-20 victory.

The Trojans then faced Indiana, the Cinderella team of the year, in the Rose Bowl. The Hoosiers were directed by former Yale mentor John Pont, then in his second year at Indiana University. He had brought his team to the championship from the cellar the year before.

Indiana was the sentimental favorite and had a brilliant quarterback in sophomore Harry Gonso. But it took more than sentiment and Gonso to halt Simpson, who scored both of the Southern California touchdowns as the Trojans won, 14-3.

* * * *

One of the wildest finishes of the season featured the game between the favored Tennessee Vols and Oklahoma in the 1968 Orange Bowl. The Sooners started with a rush as Bob Warmack, known as "The Worm" because of his elusive running, scored on three long dashes to give his team a 19-0 half-time lead.

The Vols quickly came back with two touchdowns as the second half opened; Karl Kremser, a slender soccer-style kicker,

195

booted a 24-yarder, and Tennessee had 17 points. As the fourth quarter opened, an intercepted pass by defensive back Bob Stephenson put the Sooners ahead 26-17. Only four minutes remained when the hardy Tennesseeans put on another scoring drive to cut the lead to 26 to 24. The Vols got one more chance but their drive was halted on the Oklahoma 43 with 14 seconds left. Kremser, who had kicked 10 of 15 previous attempts during the season, came in once more.

A charging Sooner line hurried the kick, however, and it sailed wide by a scant two feet, to spoil one of the great comebacks of the season as Oklahoma won 26-24.

*   *   *   *

One brief change in the rules helped expand scoring by 14 per cent to make 1968 one of the most interesting and highest scoring seasons in the game's first one hundred years. The change made it mandatory to stop the clock after each first down. The revision added about two minutes to the length of a game and allowed more plays to be run. This brought increased scoring and heightened interest in the action.

Notre Dame was one major team that took full advantage of the new rule. The Irish set a season mark of 292 first downs or 29.2 per game, and established another record of 909 offensive plays in one season. Missouri set a single game standard of 111 plays against Colorado.

O.J. Simpson had his finest season as a senior in 1968. It is difficult to associate the tall, swift-running workhorse of the Trojan backfield with skinny little Orenthal James Simpson, who wore leg braces as a child because of a calcium deficiency. Nicknamed "Pencil Legs" by the neighborhood kids in his native San Francisco, he grew up to overcome his handicap. He became a 9.3 sprinter in track and an All-America halfback as well.

Asked how he solved his physical problem, O.J. modestly replied, "I guess I was just lucky. Aside from the legs I was normal enough."

One of his greatest days was at Minnesota on a rainy Saturday in 1968. All he did was score four touchdowns and gain a total of 365 yards rushing and catching passes.

196

O. J. Simpson, USC back, overcame a physical handicap on his way to All-America honors.

"Who can ever do better than that?" asked an awestruck reporter of Trojan coach John McKay.

"Simpson," replied McKay instantly.

Despite his tremendous performances, his last regular college game saw him held to a mere 55 yards as Notre Dame and USC battled to a 21-21 thriller. He was destined for still another disappointment in his final appearance — against Ohio State in the Rose Bowl.

President-elect Nixon was among the 102,000 spectators who got their thrills early when Ohio State and USC clashed on January 1, 1969. USC moved to a 3-0 lead on Ron Ayala's field goal. Then Simpson broke off left tackle on a darting 80-yard run for a touchdown to put the Trojans further ahead, 10-0.

But Ohio State's sophomore quarterback, young Rex Kern, kept his cool. He moved his team 69 yards in 13 plays that sent fullback Jim Otis across to score, and soon a 26-yard field goal by Ohio's Jim Roman knotted the count at 10-10. In the third period Roman put his team in front 13-10, and they were never headed.

The Buckeye defense checked Simpson, and a pair of fumbles, one by O.J., brought a 27-16 victory to Ohio State.

Simpson wept over his error but graciously congratulated the victors. After all, he had done everything one man could do as he rushed for 171 yards and caught eight passes for 85 more. His touchdown run, a thing of sheer running artistry, was worth the price of admission alone.

Penn State extended its winning streak to 19 in two seasons by defeating the Kansas Jayhawks in one of the most dramatic and unusual finishes in the 35-year history of the Orange Bowl. Coach Joe Patterno's gritty team trailed 14 to 13 in the final moments of the contest. They had scored their second touchdown, only to fail

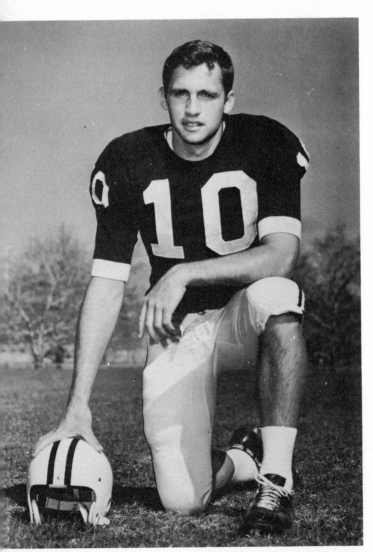

Brian Dowling figured every point scored by Ya in the famous 29-29 tie w Harvard in 1968.

in a two-point conversion attempt. There was an official huddle when it was discovered Kansas had had 12 men on the field during the play. With the crowd already streaming out of the stadium, Penn State tried again and this time the attempt was successful for a 15 to 14 victory. Many fans did not learn until they saw the result in the newspapers or heard it on the radio, that Penn State had won.

* * * *

Perhaps the year's greatest thriller, however, was not a bowl game, but appropriately enough, a contest between those two ancient Ivy League rivals, Yale and Harvard, who had so much to do with the early development of football. To begin with, it was the first year since 1909 that both teams had entered their traditional fray unbeaten and untied.

Yale started fast to lead by as many as 22 points, guided by quarterback Brian Dowling, Frank Merriwell's modern counterpart. Dowling figured in every Eli point as he ran for two touchdowns, passed for another, added one conversion point and held the ball on three other successful extra point attempts.

But Harvard also had its hero in Frank Champi, a reserve quarterback. All the fired-up Crimson back did was to pass for three touchdowns, a two pointer, and then throw an eight-yard scoring pass as time ran out on the final play. It took 15 minutes to clear the field for the extra point attempt as Yale still led, 29-27.

Then Champi joined the Crimson's great heroes of past Yale-Harvard struggles by passing to end Pete Varney for two extra points that made the final score 29-29.

Next day, the *Crimson,* Harvard's daily newspaper proudly headlined the story: "Harvard Beats Yale, 29-29." The contest was a fitting finale for the first century of college football.

* * * *

The 1969 season began the second hundred years of college football with a bang. Ohio State was the nation's top team as the schedule opened, but Texas was No. 1 when it closed. The Texans were named by President Nixon and the sportswriters' poll to that place despite the protests of Penn State followers, whose team was unbeaten in three years.

College football attendance showed an increase for the 16th straight season as it reached a record 27,626,160. Ohio State was the national leader for the 12th consecutive year with an average attendance of 86,235 for five home games.

The two largest single game crowds during the regular schedule were at Ann Arbor where the Michigan-Ohio State game attracted 103,588 fans, and the annual Army-Navy classic in Philadelphia which was attended by 102,000 spectators.

Two significant changes occurred during the season. One was the scuttling of the once popular single-wing attack by Princeton, its last major exponent. The Tigers abandoned the formation in favor of the modern slot-T and won a share of the Ivy League crown along with Yale and Dartmouth.

The second was a surprise move by Notre Dame authorities in lifting a 45-year ban on post-season competition to allow the Irish to play Texas in the Cotton Bowl. Not since 1925, when the Four Horsemen defeated Stanford in the Rose Bowl, had Notre Dame played beyond the regular season.

Upsets and thrillers marked 1969 from start to finish. Aside from a number of regular season shockers, three of the four major bowl games featured triumphs for the underdog.

Among the stunning reverses was Michigan's 24-12 conquest of Ohio State on the last day of the Big Ten season. The victory snapped a 22-game winning streak for Ohio and ruined their chance for a second straight national championship. It sent the Wolverines to the Rose Bowl and helped new coach Glenn (Bo) Schembechler to Coach-of-the-Year honors in his first season at Ann Arbor.

Schembechler came to Michigan from Miami University at Oxford, Ohio, where he amassed a six-year winning record. Ironically, he had coached Ohio State's line for five years under Woody Hayes before going to Miami.

Michigan and Schembechler did not fare so well, however, in the Rose Bowl against Southern California. Schembechler was hospitalized with a heart attack three hours before the game which the USC Trojans won 10-3. Each side scored field goals early in the game before a 33-yard scoring pass, Jimmy Jones to Bob Chandler, produced the only touchdown of the contest. The loss was Michigan's first in five Rose Bowl games, and it was Southern Cal's fourth straight appearance, for a new Bowl record.

The Texas Longhorns staged a pair of rousing comeback battles to gain the national championship. In their final game of the season against Arkansas at Fayetteville, Arkansas, with President Nixon in the stands, they found themselves trailing the Razorbacks 14-0 in the final quarter. Dejected Longhorn fans sat crushed and silent as they saw their title hopes fade. They forgot their team had spotted Oklahoma a similar lead a few weeks earlier and still won, 27-17. But James (Slick) Street, the gambling little Texas quarterback did not forget. When all of his pass receivers were covered, he legged it 42 yards to score, added two conversion points with another thrust, and cut the Arkansas lead 14 to 8.

Moments later an intercepted Razorback pass gave Street another chance. This time he hurled a 44-yard pass to the Arkansas 13, and two plays later halfback Jim Bertelsen reached the end zone. With the score tied at 14-14, place-kicker Happy Feller kicked the extra point and the Texans squeaked through 15-14. In the final seconds a desperation Arkansas pass was intercepted by Tom Campbell, son of an assistant Texas coach, and the happy Longhorn fans charged at the goal posts.

President Nixon presented Texas with a plaque emblematic of the national title afterward and there were protests from Penn State followers whose Nittany Lions boasted a 29-game undefeated streak.

Although favored over Notre Dame in the 34th annual Cotton Bowl at Dallas, the gritty Texans had to come from behind again to win the most dramatic bowl game of the post-season schedule.

As they had in the Arkansas game, Texas used the same shooting script against the Irish. Notre Dame took a 10-0 second quarter lead, chiefly as the result of quarterback Joe Theismann's 54-yard bomb to receiver Tom Gatewood. A stiff battle of lines followed, with the lighter Texans driving for two touchdowns powered by fullback Steve Worster, to forge ahead 14-10 in the fourth quarter.

Then the slender Theismann got into the act again. He fired a 24-yard scoring pass to Jim Yoder as the Irish regained the lead, 17-14.

The Texans had their replay script ready. They hit the Notre Dame 20 on fourth down with two yards to go. Unwilling to settle for a possible tie on a field goal, Coach Darrell Royal ordered a run that squeezed out a first down. Three plays later Texas faced the same situation. This time Street pitched a low pass that Cotton Speyrer barely snared on the two. There were exactly 68 seconds left when halfback Billy Dale dove into the end zone. The Irish fought back on two passes by Theismann to reach the Longhorns 38. Then Tom Campbell, The Texas ballhawk, repeated his Arkansas interception, and the Longhorns had won the Cotton Bowl, 21-17, the No. 1 rating and their school's 500th football victory.

Later President Nixon telephoned his congratulations from Washington. He asked Royal if he had considered a field goal on those two final fourth-down situations.

"Only fleetingly," admitted the Texas coach. "I believe that if a champion is going out, he ought to be carried out feet first."

Texas' fine season was marred only when safety man Fred Steinmark had a cancerous left leg amputated after the Arkansas game. Three weeks later he stood braced on his aluminum crutches along the sideline to inspire his mates against Notre Dame.

Although the sportswriters and broadcasters voted for Texas, second-ranked Penn State stretched its undefeated string to 30 games and its winning streak to 22 by whipping Missouri 10-3 in the Orange Bowl. After the game, Missouri coach Dan Devine said graciously, "If I had a vote, I'd vote for a tie between Penn State and Texas — but never Penn State second."

CHAPTER 13

College Football—
An American Heritage

SINCE THAT CRISP NOVEMBER DAY in 1869 when
Rutgers and Princeton met in the first intercollegiate football game,
an estimated 2½ million players have competed down through the
years while more than 750 million spectators cheered them on.
These figures should dispel any doubts about how Americans feel
toward the college game.

Despite its phenomenal growth, or perhaps, because of it intercollegiate football has not been without serious problems. Many
educators feel that it has been emphasized far beyond its values to
the total educational scheme. They contend that the line between
college and outright professional football has grown exceedingly
thin due to high-powered recruiting and competition for the sports
dollar.

No less an authority than H. O. (Fritz) Crisler, former chairman of the NCAA Football Rules Committee and a lifetime member of the group, is one of those concerned: "I don't think recruiting
in universities should reach the point where schools are simply
represented by pro teams, or hired players."

The Ivy League, as we have seen, recognized this danger as far back as 1956 when it engaged in a de-emphasis program. For a time attendance dwindled, but it started back again as teams improved despite the lack of high-powered recruiting. Certainly no more thrilling game was ever played than the now famous 29-29 tie between Yale and Harvard in 1969.

But almost everywhere else there is real concern about mounting costs of college athletic programs that have assumed staggering proportions. Crisler pointed out that the last time he checked recruiting figures a few years back, more than 17 million dollars had been expended across the country and the cost was still going up.

More schools may be forced to drop football, or limit aid only to football or basketball players, and let other sports shift for themselves.

With this situation in mind, "the football club" idea began to find favor in 1964 among schools where the varsity sport had been dropped. Such universities as Fordham, New York University and Georgetown began the movement which has spread to other schools.

Rivalry among club and intramural teams is as keen as among those engaging in soccer, Rugby or lacrosse, but they do not threaten to replace the varsity sport. They do, however, provide youths who have neither the inclination nor the physique for regulation football a healthy form of competition — and there is no recruiting.

Only time will tell about the future of the intercollegiate game as it moves into its second century. Football had to survive many obstacles in its first one hundred years but hard and constructive thinking remedied many unfortunate situations. The brains, the know-how and the incentives are still there.

Intercollegiate football is too great a game, too much a part of our national heritage to be spoiled or abandoned.

Its good points far outweigh its evils as the next century dawns.

Appendix

THE TEAMS AND THEIR NICKNAMES

Alabama, University of —
The Crimson Tide
Arizona, University of —
The Wildcats
Arkansas, University of —
The Razorbacks
Auburn University —
The Tigers or *The Plainsmen*
Baylor University — *The Bears*
Boston University — *The Terriers*
Brown University —
The Bears or *The Bruins*
California, University of
(at Berkeley) —
The Golden Bears
California University of
(at Los Angeles) —
UCLA or *The Bruins*
Centre College —
The Colonials or
The Prayin' Colonels
Chicago, University of —
The Maroons
Cincinnati, University of —
The Bearcats
Clemson University — *The Tigers*
Colgate University —
The Red Raiders
Colorado, University of —
The Buffaloes
Columbia University — *The Lions*
Cornell University — *The Big Red*
Dartmouth College —*The Indians*

Detroit, University of —
The Titans
Duke University —
The Blue Devils
Florida, University of —
The Fighting Gators or
The Gators
Fordham University — *The Rams*
George Washington University —
The Colonials
Georgetown University —
The Hoyas
Georgia Institute of Technology
(Georgia Tech) —
The Yellowjackets
Georgia, University of —
The Bulldogs
Harvard University —
The Crimson
Holy Cross College —
The Crusaders
Houston, University of —
The Cougars
Illinois, University of —
The Fighting Illini or
The Illini
Indiana University —
The Fightin' Hoosiers or
The Hoosiers
Iowa, University of —
The Hawkeyes
Kansas, University of —
The Jayhawks
Kentucky, University of —
The Wildcats

Lafayette College — *The Leopards*
Louisiana State University —
The Tigers or *LSU*
Maryland, University of —
The Terrapins or *The Terps*
Miami (Fla.) University of —
The Hurricanes
Miami University (Oxford, O) —
The Redskins
Michigan State University —
The Spartans
Michigan, University of —
The Wolverines
Minnesota, University of —
The Gophers
Mississippi, University of —
Ole Miss or *The Rebels*
Missouri, University of —
The Tigers
Nebraska, University of —
The Cornhuskers
New York University —
NYU or *The Violets*
Northwestern University —
The Wildcats
Notre Dame, University of —
The Fighting Irish or *The Irish*
Ohio State University, The —
The Buckeyes
Oklahoma University of —
The Sooners
Pennsylvania State University —
Penn State or
The Nittany Lions
Pennsylvania, University of —
The Quakers
Pittsburgh, University of —
The Panthers
Princeton University —
The Tigers
Purdue University —
The Boilermakers

Rice University — *The Owls*
Rutgers University —
The Scarlet Knights or
The Scarlet
Southern Methodist University —
The Mustangs
Stanford University — *The Indians*
Syracuse University —
The Orange or
The Orangemen
Temple University —
The Owls or *The Templars*
Tennessee, University of —
The Volunteers or *The Vols*
Texas A. & M. University —
The Aggies
Texas Christian University —
The Horned Frogs
Texas, University of —
The Longhorns
Tulane University —
The Green Wave
U.S. Military Academy (Army) —
The Cadets or
The Black Knights
U.S. Naval Academy (Navy) —
The Midshipmen
Washington, University of —
The Huskies
Washington and Jefferson College
— *The Presidents*
Washington and Lee University —
The Generals
Washington University
(St. Louis, Mo.) —
The Bears
West Virginia University —
The Mountaineers
Wisconsin, University of —
The Badgers
Yale University —
The Elis, The Blues or
The Bulldogs

THE ALL-TIME ALL-AMERICA TEAMS

Selection of an All-Time All-America team is a fascinating but extremely difficult task. It has been tried many times although the final result seems to come out pretty much the same. The greatest early players are still great, and probably would be among the best today. In 1951 the Associated Press polled its member sportswriters and broadcasters to select an all-time team, and in 1969 the Football Writers Association of America chose two teams — one based upon the first 50 years, from 1869 to 1919, and the other from 1920 through 1969. Since the football writers' choice is more inclusive, these two 50-year teams are presented here:

1869-1919

Huntington Hardwick (end)	Harvard University
Frank Hinkey (end)	Yale University
Wilbur (Fats) Henry (tackle)	Washington & Jefferson College
Josh Cody (tackle)	Vanderbilt University
W. W. (Pudge) Heffelfinger (guard)	Yale University
Truxton Hare (guard)	University of Pennsylvania
Adolph "Germany" Schultz (center)	University of Michigan
Walter Eckersall (quarterback)	University of Chicago
Willie Heston (halfback)	University of Michigan
Elmer Oliphant (halfback)	U.S. Military Academy and Purdue University
Jim Thorpe (fullback)	Carlisle School for Indians

1919-1969

Don Hutson (end)	University of Alabama
Bennie Oosterbaan (end)	University of Michigan
Frank (Bruiser) Kinard (tackle)	University of Mississippi
Bronko Nagurski (tackle)	University of Minnesota
Jim Parker (guard)	The Ohio State University
Bob Suffridge (guard)	University of Tennessee
Mel Hein (center)	Washington State University
Sammy Baugh (quarterback)	Texas Christian University
Jay Berwanger (halfback)	University of Chicago
Harold (Red) Grange (halfback)	University of Illinois
Ernie Nevers (fullback)	Stanford University

COACH OF THE YEAR AWARD

1935	Lynn Waldorf, Northwestern	1954	Henry (Red) Sanders, UCLA
1936	Dick Harlow, Harvard	1955	Duffy Daugherty, Michigan State
1937	Edward Mylin, Lafayette	1956	Bowden Wyatt, Tennessee
1938	Bill Kern, Carnegie Tech	1957	Woody Hayes, Ohio State
1939	Eddie Anderson, Iowa	1958	Paul Dietzel, LSU
1940	Clark Shaughnessy, Stanford	1959	Ben Schwartzwalder, Syracuse
1941	Frank Leahy, Notre Dame	1960	Murray Warmath, Minnesota
1942	Bill Alexander, Georgia Tech	1961	Paul (Bear) Bryant, Alabama
1943	Amos Alonzo Stagg, Pacific	1962	John McKay, Southern Cal
1944	Carroll Widdoes, Ohio State	1963	Darrell Royal, Texas
1945	Bo McMillin, Indiana	1964	Frank Broyles, Arkansas and
1946	Earl (Red) Blaik, Army		Ara Parseghian, Notre Dame
1947	Fritz Crisler, Michigan	1965	Tommy Prothro, UCLA
1948	Bennie Oosterbaan, Michigan	1966	Tom Cahill, Army
1949	Bud Wilkinson, Oklahoma	1967	John Pont, Indiana
1950	Charlie Caldwell, Princeton	1968	Joe Paterno, Penn State
1951	Chuck Taylor, Stanford	1969	Glenn (Bo) Schembechler,
1952	Biggie Munn, Michigan State		Michigan
1953	Jim Tatum, Maryland		

MOST HEAD-COACHING VICTORIES

		Victories			Victories
1	Amos Alonzo Stagg	314	17	Lynn (Pappy) Waldorf	170
2	Glenn (Pop) Warner	313	18	Earl (Red) Blaik	166
3	Warren Woodson	239	19	Bobby Dodd	165
4	Jess Neely	207	20	Frank Howard	165
5	Eddie Anderson	201	21	Don Faurot	164
6	Dana Bible	198	22	Ossie Solem	162
7	Dan McGugin	197	23	*Ben Schwartzwalder	160
8	Fielding Yost	196	24	*Woody Hayes	158
9	Howard Jones	194	25	Francis Schmidt	158
10	*Paul (Bear) Bryant	193	26	Edward Robinson	156
11	John Heisman	185	27	Morley Jennings	155
12	Carl Snavely	180	28	Ray Morrison	155
13	Gil Dobie	179	29	Bennie Owen	155
14	*John Vaught	178	30	Matty Bell	154
15	Bob Neyland	173	31	Lou Little	151
16	Wallace Wade	171			

*Active coach.

HEISMAN MEMORIAL TROPHY

(Honors outstanding college football player. Presented by Downtown Athletic Club of New York)

Year	Player, College, Pos.	Year	Player, College, Pos.
1935	Jay Berwanger, Chicago, HB	1941	Bruce Smith, Minnesota, HB
1936	Larry Kelley, Yale, E	1942	Frank Sinkwich, Georgia, HB
1937	Clint Frank, Yale, HB	1943	Angelo Bertelli, Notre Dame, QB
1938	Davey O'Brien, TCU, QB	1944	Les Horvath, Ohio State, QB
1939	Nile Kinnick, Iowa, HB	1945	Doc Blanchard, Army, FB
1940	Tom Harmon, Michigan, HB	1946	Glenn Davis, Army, HB

Year	Player, College, Pos.	Year	Player, College, Pos.
1947	John Lujack, Notre Dame, QB	1959	Billy Cannon, LSU, HB
1948	Doak Walker, SMU, HB	1960	Joe Bellino, Navy, HB
1949	Leon Hart, Notre Dame, E	1961	Ernie Davis, Syracuse, HB
1950	Vic Janowicz, Ohio State, HB	1962	Terry Baker, Oregon St., QB
1951	Dick Kazmaier, Princeton, HB	1963	Roger Staubach, Navy, QB
1952	Billy Vessels, Oklahoma, HB	1964	John Huarte, Notre Dame, QB
1953	John Lattner, Notre Dame, HB	1965	Mike Garrett, Southern Cal, HB
1954	Alan Ameche, Wisconsin, FB	1966	Steve Spurrier, Florida, QB
1955	Howard Cassady, Ohio State, HB	1967	Gary Beban, UCLA, QB
1956	Paul Hornung, Notre Dame, QB	1968	O. J. Simpson, Southern Cal, HB
1957	John Crow, Texas A&M, HB	1969	Steve Owens, Oklahoma, HB
1958	Pete Dawkins, Army, HB		

OUTLAND TROPHY

(Honors outstanding interior lineman, selected by the Football Writers' Association of America)

Year	Player, College, Pos.	Year	Player, College, Pos.
1946	George Connor, Notre Dame, T	1958	Zeke Smith, Auburn, G
1947	Joe Steffy, Army, G	1959	Max McGee, Duke, T
1948	Bill Fischer, Notre Dame, G	1960	Tom Brown, Minnesota, G
1949	Ed Bagdon, Michigan St., G	1961	Merlin Olsen, Utah State, T
1950	Bob Gain, Kentucky, T	1962	Bobby Bell, Minnesota, T
1951	Jim Weatherall, Oklahoma, T	1963	Scott Appleton, Texas, T
1952	Dick Modzelewski, Maryland, T	1964	Steve DeLong, Tennessee, T
1953	J. D. Roberts, Oklahoma, G	1965	Tommy Nobis, Texas, G
1954	Bill Brooks, Arkansas, G	1966	Loyd Phillips, Arkansas, T
1955	Calvin Jones, Iowa, G	1967	Ron Yary, Southern Cal, T
1956	Jim Parker, Ohio State, G	1968	Bill Stanfill, Georgia, T
1957	Alex Karras, Iowa, T	1969	Mike Reid, Penn State, T

LONGEST WINNING STREAKS

Wins	Team	Years	Ended by	Score
47	Oklahoma	1953-57	Notre Dame	7-0
39	Washington	1908-14	Oregon State	0-0
37	Yale	1890-93	Princeton	6-0
37	Yale	1887-89	Princeton	10-0
34	Pennsylvania	1894-96	Lafayette	6-4
31	Oklahoma	1948-50	Kentucky	*13-7
31	Pittsburgh	1914-18	Cleveland Naval Res.	10-9
31	Pennsylvania	1896-98	Harvard	10-0
29	Michigan	1901-03	Minnesota	6-6
28	Michigan State	1950-53	Purdue	6-0
27	Nebraska	1901-04	Colorado	6-0
26	Cornell	1921-24	Williams	14-7
26	Michigan	1903-05	Chicago	2-0
25	Michigan	1946-49	Army	21-7
25	Army	1944-46	Notre Dame	0-0
25	Southern Cal	1931-33	Oregon State	0-0
24	Princeton	1949-52	Pennsylvania	13-7
24	Minnesota	1903-05	Wisconsin	16-12
24	Yale	1894-95	Boston AC	0-0

*Streak ended in bowl game.

Wins	Team	Years	Ended by	Score
24	Harvard	1890-91	Yale	10-0
24	Yale	1882-84	Princeton	0-0
23	Harvard	1901-02	Yale	23-0
22	Arkansas	1963-65	LSU	*14-7
22	Tennessee	1937-39	Southern Cal	*14-0
22	Harvard	1912-14	Penn State	13-13
22	Yale	1904-06	Princeton	0-0
22	Ohio State	1967-69	Michigan	24-12
22	Penn State	**1967-69		
21	Notre Dame	1946-48	Southern Cal	14-14
21	Minnesota	1933-36	Northwestern	6-0
21	Colorado	1908-12	Colo. State U.	21-0
21	Pennsylvania	1903-05	Lafayette	6-6
21	Yale	1900-01	Army	5-5
21	Harvard	1898-99	Yale	0-0
20	Tennessee	1950-51	Maryland	*28-13
20	Notre Dame	1929-31	Northwestern	0-0
20	Alabama	1924-26	Stanford	*7-7
20	Iowa	1920-23	Illinois	9-6
20	Notre Dame	1919-21	Iowa	10-7

*Streak ended in bowl game.
**Undefeated going into 1970 season.

THE BOWL GAMES

The first bowl game was played at Pasadena, California, on New Year's Day, 1902, as part of a publicity stunt for its annual Tournament of Roses. It was not much of a contest as Michigan defeated Stanford, 49-0. Although it was successful financially, the second game was not played until 1916 when Brown University and Washington State College were invited to participate by the tournament group. Since then the event has gradually evolved into a million dollar plus affair, especially since radio and television entered the picture. In 1922 the game got a real boost with the construction of the Rose Bowl stadium, seating 52,000 spectators. The original structure, a horse shoe and not a bowl, later became enclosed and enlarged to seat 102,000 spectators.

As the game gained in stature, it became a test between Pacific Coast teams and those of other sections, the tournament committee deciding the invitations. Many schools had non-bowl rules at first, but these gradually loosened, and in 1946 the Pacific Coast Conference and the Big Ten formed a pact between their two loops that still exists.

In 1933 the city of Miami, Florida, sponsored a Palm festival that was changed to the Orange Bowl the next year. The Sugar Bowl at New Orleans followed in 1935, and the Cotton Bowl series began at Dallas in 1937. The Gator Bowl followed these four and for a time bowl games flourished everywhere until the National Collegiate Athletic Association formulated regulations for its members and the slate of 47 bowls was reduced by half. Notre Dame played Stanford in the Rose Bowl in 1925 but then set a non-bowl rule until 1969 when it relaxed the measure to send the team against Texas in the Cotton Bowl.

MAJOR BOWL GAMES RESULTS

Rose Bowl (Pasadena)

1902—Michigan 49, Stanford 0
1916—Washington St. 14, Brown 0
1917—Oregon 14, Pennsylvania 0
1918—Mare Island 19, Camp Lewis 7
1919—Great Lakes 17, Mare Island 0
1920—Harvard 7, Oregon 6
1921—California 28, Ohio State 0
1922—Wash. & Jeff. 0, California 0
1923—Southern Cal 14, Penn State 3
1924—Navy 14, Washington 14
1925—Notre Dame 27, Stanford 10
1926—Alabama 20, Washington 19
1927—Alabama 7, Stanford 7
1928—Stanford 7, Pittsburgh 6
1929—Georgia Tech 8, California 7
1930—Southern Cal 47, Pittsburgh 14
1931—Alabama 24, Washington St. 0
1932—Southern Cal 21, Tulane 12
1933—Southern Cal 35, Pittsburgh 0
1934—Columbia 7, Stanford 0
1935—Alabama 29, Stanford 13
1936—Stanford 7, SMU 0
1937—Pittsburgh 21, Washington 0
1938—California 13, Alabama 0
1939—Southern Cal 7, Duke 3
1940—Southern Cal 14, Tennessee 0
1941—Stanford 21, Nebraska 13
1942—Oregon St. 20, Duke 16
        (at Durham)

1943—Georgia 9, UCLA 0
1944—Southern Cal 29, Washington 0
1945—Southern Cal 25, Tennessee 0
1946—Alabama 34, Southern Cal 14
1947—Illinois 45, UCLA 14
1948—Michigan 49, Southern Cal 0
1949—Northwestern 20, California 14
1950—Ohio State 17, California 14
1951—Michigan 14, California 6
1952—Illinois 40, Stanford 7
1953—Southern Cal 7, Wisconsin 0
1954—Michigan St. 28, UCLA 20
1955—Ohio State 20, Southern Cal 7
1956—Michigan St. 17, UCLA 14
1957—Iowa 35, Oregon St. 19
1958—Ohio State 10, Oregon 7
1959—Iowa 38, California 12
1960—Washington 44, Wisconsin 8
1961—Washington 17, Minnesota 7
1962—Minnesota 21, UCLA 3
1963—Southern Cal 42, Wisconsin 37
1964—Illinois 17, Washington 7
1965—Michigan 34, Oregon St. 7
1966—UCLA 14, Michigan St. 12
1967—Purdue 14, Southern Cal 13
1968—Southern Cal 14, Indiana 3
1969—Ohio State 27, Southern Cal 16
1970—Southern Cal 10, Michigan 3

Orange Bowl (Miami)

1933—Miami (Fla.) 7, Manhattan 0
1934—Duquesne 33, Miami (Fla.) 7
1935—Bucknell 26, Miami (Fla.) 0
1936—Catholic U. 20, Mississippi 19
1937—Duquesne 13, Miss. State 12
1938—Auburn 6, Michigan St. 0
1939—Tennessee 17, Oklahoma 0
1940—Georgia Tech 21, Missouri 7
1941—Miss. State 14, Georgetown 7
1942—Georgia 40, TCU 26
1943—Alabama 37, Boston Col. 21
1944—LSU 19, Texas A&M 14
1945—Tulsa 26, Georgia Tech 12
1946—Miami (Fla.) 13, Holy Cross 6
1947—Rice 8, Tennessee 0
1948—Georgia Tech 20, Kansas 14
1949—Texas 41, Georgia 28
1950—Santa Clara 21, Kentucky 13
1951—Clemson 15, Miami (Fla.) 14

1952—Georgia Tech 17, Baylor 14
1953—Alabama 61, Syracuse 6
1954—Oklahoma 7, Maryland 0
1955—Duke 34, Nebraska 7
1956—Oklahoma 20, Maryland 6
1957—Colorado 27, Clemson 21
1958—Oklahoma 48, Duke 21
1959—Oklahoma 21, Syracuse 6
1960—Georgia 14, Missouri 0
1961—Missouri 21, Navy 14
1962—LSU 25, Colorado 7
1963—Alabama 17, Oklahoma 0
1964—Nebraska 13, Auburn 7
1965—Texas 21, Alabama 17
1966—Alabama 39, Nebraska 28
1967—Florida 27, Georgia Tech 12
1968—Oklahoma 26, Tennessee 24
1969—Penn State 15, Kansas 14
1970—Penn State 10, Missouri 3

Cotton Bowl (Dallas)

1937—TCU 16, Marquette 6
1938—Rice 28, Colorado 14
1939—St. Mary's 20, Texas Tech 13
1940—Clemson 6, Boston Col. 3
1941—Texas A&M 13, Fordham 12
1942—Alabama 29, Texas A&M 21
1943—Texas 14, Georgia Tech 7
1944—Randolph Field 7, Texas 7
1945—Oklahoma St. 34, TCU 0
1946—Texas 40, Missouri 27
1947—Arkansas 0, LSU 0
1948—SMU 13, Penn State 13
1949—SMU 21, Oregon 13
1950—Rice 27, North Carolina 13
1951—Tennessee 20, Texas 14
1952—Kentucky 20, TCU 7
1953—Texas 16, Tennessee 0

1954—Rice 28, Alabama 6
1955—Georgia Tech 14, Arkansas 6
1956—Mississippi 14, TCU 13
1957—TCU 28, Syracuse 27
1958—Navy 20, Rice 7
1959—TCU 0, Air Force 0
1960—Syracuse 23, Texas 14
1961—Duke 7, Arkansas 6
1962—Texas 12, Mississippi 7
1963—LSU 13, Texas 0
1964—Texas 28, Navy 6
1965—Arkansas 10, Nebraska 7
1966—LSU 14, Arkansas 7
1967—Georgia 23, SMU 9
1968—Texas A&M 20, Alabama 16
1969—Texas 36, Tennessee 13
1970—Texas 21, Notre Dame 17

Sugar Bowl (New Orleans)

1935—Tulane 20, Temple 14
1936—TCU 3, LSU 2
1937—Santa Clara 21, LSU 14
1938—Santa Clara 6, LSU 0
1939—TCU 15, Carnegie Tech 7
1940—Texas A&M 14, Tulane 13
1941—Boston Col. 19, Tennessee 13
1942—Fordham 2, Missouri 0
1943—Tennessee 14, Tulsa 7
1944—Georgia Tech 20, Tulsa 18
1945—Duke 29, Alabama 26
1946—Oklahoma St. 33, St. Mary's 13
1947—Georgia 20, North Carolina 10
1948—Texas 27, Alabama 7
1949—Oklahoma 14, North Carolina 6
1950—Oklahoma 35, LSU 0
1951—Kentucky 13, Oklahoma 7
1952—Maryland 28, Tennessee 13

1953—Georgia Tech 24, Mississippi 7
1954—Georgia Tech 42, West Virginia 19
1955—Navy 21, Mississippi 0
1956—Georgia Tech 7, Pittsburgh 0
1957—Baylor 13, Tennessee 7
1958—Mississippi 39, Texas 7
1959—LSU 7, Clemson 0
1960—Mississippi 21, LSU 0
1961—Mississippi 14, Rice 6
1962—Alabama 10, Arkansas 3
1963—Mississippi 17, Arkansas 13
1964—Alabama 12, Mississippi 7
1965—LSU 13, Syracuse 10
1966—Missouri 20, Florida 18
1967—Alabama 34, Nebraska 7
1968—LSU 20, Wyoming 13
1969—Arkansas 16, Georgia 2
1970—Mississippi 27, Arkansas 22

We wish to thank Steve Boda, Jr., and the National Collegiate Sports Services for permission to use such records in the Appendix as the Longest Winning Streaks, Most Head-Coaching Victories and for other assistance.

Thanks also to the many sports information directors for their cooperation.

Index

Adams, John, 12
Alabama, University of, 104, 138, 139, 176, 177, 178, 179, 189, 195
Albert, Frankie, 148, 149
Alcott, Clarence, 97
All-America, 49, 57, 67-71, 77-78, 79, 80, 81, 82, 83, 87, 89, 101, 102, 103, 107, 108, 109, 110, 111, 112, 116, 120, 122, 123, 124, 126, 131, 134, 135, 136, 137, 139, 145, 146, 152, 153, 155, 156, 160, 165, 173, 180, 181, 182, 185, 186, 187, 189, 207
Allen, G. C., 28
Altenburg, Kurt, 189
American Intercollegiate Football Association, 41, 42, 43, 46; Rules Committee of, 42, 47
Amherst College, 14
Anderson, Hunk, 131
Antenucci, Frank, 142
Apisa, Bob, 189
Appleton, Scott, 183
Arizona, University of, 191
Arkansas, University of, 176, 201, 202
Army, see United States Military Academy
Arnold, William, 31, 33
Associated Press Poll, 106, 171, 189
Atkins, Pop, 76
Auburn University, 76, 78, 94
Ayala, Ron, 197

Baker, Eugene V., 28, 37-39, 41, 43
Baker, Johnny, 131
Baker, Ralph (Moon), 112
Banas, Steve, 131
Barabas, Al, 137, 138
Baugh, Sammy, 140, 141
Beban, Garry, 188, 189, 195
Bellino, Joe, 181
Bell, Matty, 140, 161
Bertelsen, Jim, 201
Berwanger, Jay, 134, 135
Bierman, Bernie, 129, 133, 135, 154, 165

Big Five, 172
Big Nine, 78
Big Ten, 78, 82, 83, 97, 98, 99, 124, 131, 132, 133, 135, 152, 153, 156, 166, 168, 169, 191
Big Three, 34, 51, 72, 73, 95, 98, 100, 101
Blaik, Earl (Red), 156, 157
Blanchard, Benjamin S., 33-34
Blanchard, Felix (Doc), 156, 157, 158
Bloody Monday, 14
Booth, Albie, 110, 126
Boston College, 126, 154, 155
Boston Game, 25, 26, 28
Boston Rules, 17
Bowman, Steve, 178
Boydston, Max, 165
Brennan, Terry, 166, 184
Brewer, Charlie, 62-63
Brickley, Charlie, 101, 102, 103
British Rugby Union, 10, 37, 39
Britton, Earl, 112, 115
Brown, Gordon F., 69, 70-71
Brown, Paul, 155, 156
Brown University, 14, 121, 132, 146
Bruder, Hank (Hard Luck), 132
Brutality of football, 4, 5, 6, 11, 13-14, 24, 51-52, 64-65, 90-92, 93; crusade against, 91-92, 93
Bryant, Paul (Bear), 138, 163, 176, 177, 178, 194, 195
Buffalo, University of, 87
Burdick, Arnie, 190
Bushnell, George V., 41

Cagle, Chris, 11, 126
Cahill, Tom, 193
Calcio, 4, 5
Caldwell, Charley, 169, 170
California, University of, 67, 73, 75, 91, 168, 172
California, University of (at Los Angeles), 145, 146, 168, 171, 172, 188, 192, 195

Cambridge University, 9, 10
Camp, Walter Chauncey, 35-49, 51, 65, 67, 68, 69, 70, 71, 73, 77, 78, 79, 80, 81, 82, 83, 89, 92, 94, 95, 101, 103, 107, 108, 110, 116
Campbell, Tom, 202
Cannon, Billy, 172, 173
Carideo, Frank, 130
Carlisle, Duke, 183
Carlisle (Industrial School for Indians), 97, 103-06, 107-08, 122
Carnegie Institute of Technology, 117, 141
Cassady, Howard (Hopalong), 171
Cavanaugh, Frank (Iron Major), 126
Cavender, Regis, 192
Centre College, 110
Champi, Frank, 199
Chandler, Bob, 200
Chappuis, Bob, 159
Chicago, University of, 72, 75, 78, 79-81, 82, 83, 85, 98, 104, 134, 135, 146, 147, 168
Chicago Bears, 116, 124, 146, 147, 150, 180
Christman, Paul, 150
City College of New York, 26, 163
Clark, George, 37
Clarke, Gordon, 79
Cleveland Browns, 174
Coach of the Year Award, 83, 170, 176, 193, 200, 208
Cochems, Edward B., 96
Colgate University, 132, 133
College of the Pacific, 83
Colorado, University of, 145, 196
Columbia University, 16, 24, 25, 26-27, 41, 91, 136, 137, 138, 151, 163
Concessionary Rules, 32-33
Corbin, William H. (Pa), 56, 57
Cornell University, 26, 61, 75, 104, 105, 142, 143, 144, 145, 190
Cotton Bowl, 174, 182, 183, 194, 200, 202, 212
Coulter, Tex, 156
Crisler, Fritz, 133, 135, 137, 157, 158, 160, 163, 171, 203
Cross, Harry, 99
Crowley, Jimmy, 117, 118, 119, 141, 154
Csonka, Larry, 173, 192
Cumberland College, 76, 94-95
Curtis, Nathaniel, 38, 39

Dale, Billy, 202
Dallas, University of, 75
Dartmouth College, 119, 120, 122, 143, 144, 151, 156, 200
Dashiell, Paul, 94
Dougherty, Hugh (Duffy), 169, 189
Davis, Bill, 95
Davis, Ernie, 174
Davis, Glenn, 156, 157, 158, 159
Davis, Parke H., 62
Deland, Lorin F., 60-61

Delaware, University of, 151
Dempsey, Jack, 110, 122
DePoyster, Jerry, 191
Dersheimer, C., 27
Detroit Tigers, 121
Devine, Dan, 202
DeVore, Hugh, 184
Dietzel, Paul, 172, 173, 184, 192
Dillon, Charley, 104-05
Dixwell Latin School, 16-17, 20
Dodge, W. Earle, 34
Dorais, Gus, 98-99, 147
Dowling, Brian, 198, 199
Downs and plays, Introduction of, 47
Duke University, 138, 154, 180
Duquesne University, 163
Dyas, Bill, 176

East-West Shrine Game, 132
Eckersall, Walter, 82, 83, 85, 88
Eddy, Nick, 191
Eichenlaub, Ray, 100
Eisenhower, Dwight D., 108
Eliot, Charles William, 20, 92
Elliott, Bump, 159
Ellis, William Webb, 8-10
Eton Players, 27-28
Eton School, 7, 27-28
Evashevski, Forest, 152

Fairmont, see Wichita, University of
Faurot, Don, 150, 151, 154, 164, 174
Feller, Happy, 201
Ferguson, Bob, 171
Fertig, Craig, 186
Finley, Bob, 141
Flippin, Royce, 171
Football, 84, 86
Football, Ancient, 1-10
Football Fightum, 15, 20, 25
Football Writers' Association, 190
Fordham University, 141, 204
Forward pass, Introduction of, 41, 93, 94, 96-99
Four Horsemen, 110, 111, 112, 116, 117, 118, 119, 120, 128, 141, 200
Frank, Clint, 136, 137
Franklin Field, 79, 115, 172
Free kick, Introduction of, 22, 23, 29
Friedman, Ben, 111, 114, 120, 121
Friesell, Red, 144
Fromhart, Wally, 142

Gallarneau, Hugh, 148, 149
Garbisch, Edgar, 126
Garrett, Mike, 186
Gatewood, Tom, 201
Gator Bowl, 192
Gipp, George, 110
Georgetown University, 163, 204
Georgia, University of, 76, 94, 177
Georgia Institute of Technology, 76, 78, 94-95, 118, 122, 155

Gogolak, Charley, 190, 191
Gogolak, Pete, 191
Gonso, Harry, 195
Grange, Red, 89, 106, 110, 111, 112, 114, 115, 116, 120, 124, 128
Grant, Henry, 28
Grayson, Bobby, 138
Green Bay Packers, 139, 141
Grigas, John, 155
Groton School, 70, 101, 102
Gummere, William S., 21
Gushurst, Fred, 99

Hahn, Archie, 86
Halas, George, 124, 146, 150, 180
Halstead, William S., 28
Hamilton, Tom, 120, 154
Hamilton Park, 27, 35
Hanratty, Terry, 191
Hardin, Wayne, 181, 182
Hardwick, Huntington (Tack), 101, 102-03
Hare, T. Truxton, 68-69, 70-71
Hargett, Ed, 194
Harley, Chick, 111
Harmon, Harvey, 154
Harmon, Tom, 152, 153
Harpaston, 1-3
Harpastum, 1, 3
Harper, Jesse, 98, 100, 101
Harris, Phil, 183
Harvard Stadium, 90, 91, 103
Harvard University, 12, 14-16, 19, 20, 26, 28-34, 35, 37-41, 44, 46, 51, 52, 54, 60-63, 68, 69, 73, 74-75, 78, 91, 92, 97, 101, 102, 103, 104-06, 107, 121, 126, 172, 198, 199, 204
Haughton, Percy Duncan, 101-02, 103, 106, 107
Haughton system, 101
Haxall, John, 54
Hayes, Woody, 170, 171, 200
Heath, Leon, 165
Heffelfinger, William W. (Pudge), 57, 65-68
Heisman, John W., 76, 94
Heisman Trophy, 76, 134, 135, 152, 160, 170, 181, 185, 208
Herschberger, Clarence, 79, 80, 81
Heston, Willie, 86, 87, 89-90
Hickok, Orville, 63
Hinckey, Frank, 68, 69-70, 85, 100
Hodge, Richard M., 55
Holland, Brud, 145, 146
Holy Cross College, 154, 155, 174
Homan, Dennis, 177
Hoover, Herbert, 75
Hope, Hugh, 95
Hopkins Grammar School, 35, 36-37
Hornung, Paul, 174
Horvath, Les, 156
Housley, Wendell, 195
Hovde, Fred, 124
Howell, Dixie, 138
Huarte, John, 185

Hunt, Joel, 127
Hutson, Don, 138, 139

Illinois, University of, 75, 78, 89, 110, 111, 112, 115, 141, 153, 167, 168
Indiana University, 73, 75, 195
Iowa, University of, 75, 88, 96, 123, 124, 145, 146, 153
Ivy League, 172, 199, 200, 204

Janowicz, Vic, 167, 168
Jennings, Walter, 36
Joesting, Herb, 123
Johnson, Jimmy, 104-05
Jones, Clint, 191
Jones, Howard, 129, 131
Jones, Jimmy, 200
Jones, Ralph, 146
Jones, Tad, 126
Juday, Steve, 189

Kaiser, Dave, 169
Kansas, University of, 96, 141, 173, 179, 180, 198, 199
Kazmaier, Dick, 170, 171
Kelley, Larry, 136, 137
Kenna, Doug, 156
Kennedy, Walter, 81
Kenny, Dick, 189
Kentucky, University of, 120, 163, 176, 177
Kern, Rex, 197
Kerr, Andy, 132, 133, 165
Kimbrough, John, 145
King, Phil, 59, 78
Kinnick, Nile, 145
Kipke, Harry, 131
Kivlan, James H., 73
Kmetovic, Pete, 148, 149, 150
Kostka, Stan, 133, 135
Kreager, Carl, 167
Kremsler, Karl, 195, 196
Kuharich, Joe, 184

Lamar, Henry G. (Tilly), 54, 55
Lambert Trophy, 151, 170
Lane, Bobby, 161
Layden, Elmer, 117, 118, 119, 142
Layden, Mike, 142
Lea, Luke, 75, 76-77
Leahy, Frank, 154, 165, 166
Leggett, William J., 21
Lewis, Leland (Tiny), 120
Levias, Jerry, 194
Lindell, Steve, 193
Little, Floyd, 192
Little, George, 114
Little, Lou, 137, 151
Lom, Benny, 122
Lombardi, Vince, 141
London Football Association, 10, 17, 21, 26

Louisiana State University, 76, 172, 173
Loyola University, 150
Lujack, Johnny, 158
Lund, Francis (Pug), 133, 135

Mahan, Eddie, 101, 102, 103
Mallory, Bill, 126
Maryland, University of, 165, 174, 176
Mass formations and mass momentum
    plays, Introduction of, 56
Maxwell, Bob, 91
McAfee, George, 180
McCormick, Vance, 62
McGill University, 28-31
McIlwain, Wally, 115
McDonald, Tommy, 165
McKay, Johnny, 186, 197
McMillan, Alvin (Bo), 110, 111
Merriwell, Frank, 199
Metzger, W. E., 78
Miami University of Ohio, 184, 185, 200
Michigan, University of, 26, 72, 74-75,
    78, 81, 85, 86, 87, 88, 99, 111, 112,
    114, 120, 121, 124, 131, 132, 133,
    152, 153, 157, 159, 160, 166, 167,
    168, 169, 200, 201
Michigan State University, 88, 168, 169,
    187, 189, 191, 192
Middle Atlantic Conference, 151
Miller, Gerrit Smith, 16-20
Miller, Steve, 142
Millice, Glenn, 95
Millner, Wayne, 142
Millstead, Century, 126
Minnesota, University of, 67, 73, 75, 78,
    104, 122, 123, 124, 125, 129, 133,
    148, 150, 153, 166, 196
Missouri, University of, 73, 150, 151,
    174, 179, 196, 202
Mitchell, Jack, 165
Moffat, Alexander, 52, 54
Mohler, Orv, 131
Montgomery, Cliff, 137, 138
Morrison, Ray, 127
Mullins, Moon, 130
Munn, Clarence (Biggie), 168, 169
Murphy, Mike, 70
Murphy, Russ, 144
Murrell, Johnny, 126
Myers, Denny, 154
Myers, Dutch, 140, 161

Nagurski, Bronko, 122, 123, 124, 125
Namath, Joe, 177, 178, 179
National Collegiate Athletic Association,
    92, 162, 166, 176, 191, 203; Rules
    Committee of, 117, 122, 129, 133,
    163, 175
National Football League, 135
Navy, see United States Naval Academy
Nebraska, University of, 104, 112, 118,
    147, 148, 149, 150, 179, 189
Neighbors, Billy, 177
Nelson, Davey, 151

Nevers, Ernie, 70, 119
Newell, Marshall (Ma), 68, 69
Newman, Harry, 131
New York Jets, 177, 178, 179
New York University, 26, 111, 121, 132,
    141, 204
Neyland, General Bob, 129
Nicknames of teams, 205-06
North Carolina, University of, 76-77, 94
North Carolina State University, 177,
    178
Northwestern University, 75, 78, 91,
    104, 112, 118, 120, 130, 131, 132,
    167, 168, 184, 185
Notre Dame, University of, 73, 85, 98-
    101, 110, 111, 112, 117, 118, 123,
    130, 131, 141, 142, 143, 147, 156,
    158, 159, 163, 165, 166, 184, 185,
    186, 191, 192, 195, 196, 197, 200,
    201, 202
Notre Dame system, 101

O'Dea, Pat, 78-79, 80, 81
Ohio State University, 67, 73, 75, 88,
    104, 111, 141, 142, 143, 155, 167,
    168, 170, 171, 197, 198, 199, 200
Oklahoma, University of, 135, 163, 164,
    165, 166, 174, 178, 179, 195, 196
Old Bigside, 8, 9
Oneida Football Club, 17-20
Oneida Football Monument, 19, 20
Oosterbaan, Ben, 111, 114, 120, 121,
    153, 160
Open game, Introduction of, 56
Orange Bowl, 189, 195, 198, 202, 211
Ortmann, Chuck, 167
Oregon, University of, 73, 172
Oregon State University, 154, 172, 195
Otis, Jim, 197
Oxford University, 9, 10

Pacific Coast Conference, 146, 171
Pacific Eight Conference, 172
Palmer Stadium, 23, 90
Parilli, Babe, 163
Parseghian, Ara, 184, 185, 186, 191
Patterno, Joe, 198
Pennsylvania, University of, 54, 63, 64,
    69, 70, 71, 72, 73, 77, 78, 79, 81, 91,
    104, 115, 116, 130, 153, 170
Pennsylvania State University, 104, 132,
    172, 174, 198, 199, 202
Perez, Ines, 194
Pierce, Captain Palmer E., 92
Pilney, Andy, 142
Pinckert, Ernie, 131
Pittsburgh, University of, 104, 108, 129,
    130, 132, 133, 135, 141, 172, 174
Platanistas, 13
Platoons, 158, 162, 184, 186
Pliska, Joe, 99
Poe brothers, 71-72
Poe, Edgar Allen, 52, 72
Pollard, Fritz, 146

Polo Grounds, 46, 51
Pond, Raymond (Ducky), 126
Pont, John, 195
Poole, Barney, 156
Potter, Jotham, 34
Princeton University, 12, 16, 20-23, 24,
    25, 26-27, 34, 41, 42, 44, 46, 50, 51,
    52-55, 59, 61, 70, 71-72, 73, 74-75,
    77, 78, 90, 91, 94, 118, 133, 136, 137,
    169, 170, 171, 172, 190, 200, 203
Purdue University, 73, 75, 124, 132,
    163, 168, 192
Pyle, C. C. (Cash and Carry), 116

Racine College, 74
Reagan, Francis, 153
Remington, Frederic, 48, 58, 63
Rice, Grantland, 67, 103, 108, 112, 116,
    124, 131, 176
Rickey, Branch, 146
Riegels, Roy, 122
Robeson, Paul, 146
Robinson, Bradbury, 95-96, 99
Robinson, Jackie, 145, 146
Rockne, Knute, 98, 99, 100-01, 111,
    117, 118, 119, 123, 130, 138, 147,
    158, 166
Roger, David, 28
Roman, Jim, 197
Roosevelt, Theodore, 91, 93, 95
Roper, Bob, 171
Rose Bowl, 88, 118, 122, 132, 136, 137,
    138, 139, 141, 147, 148, 149, 152,
    154, 159, 167, 168, 187, 192, 195,
    197, 200, 201, 211
Rosenberg, Aaron, 131
Rossides, Gene, 151
Royal, Darrell, 165, 175, 181, 182, 202
Rugby, 3, 9-10, 25, 26, 28-30, 32-34, 35,
    37, 39, 41, 42-43, 45, 46, 52, 56, 64,
    74, 91, 204
Rugby School, 7, 8-10, 25
Running attack, Introduction of, 8-10
Runyon, Damon, 138
Rutgers Stadium, 23
Rutgers University, 16, 20-23, 24, 25,
    26-27, 33, 74, 146, 151, 203

St. Louis University, 95, 96, 97
St. Mary's College, 163
Sanders, Henry (Red), 171
San José Normal College, 85, 86
Savoldi, Joe, 130
Sayers, Gale, 179, 180
Scarbeth, Jack, 174
Schembechler, Glenn (Bo), 200
Schaff, David Schley, 25
Schmidt, Francis A., 141, 142
Schneider, Jack, 96, 99
Scholl, Pop, 143, 144
Schulte, Henry, 89
Schultz, Adolph G. (Germany), 89

Schwartz, Marchie, 131
Scrimmage, 30, 43-44, 45, 46, 49, 56,
    64, 67, 90, 92, 93, 94
Schwartzwalder, Ben, 173
Scrum, 30, 43, 44, 45
Seven Blocks of Granite, 141
Seven Mules, 117, 118
Sewanee, University of, 75-78
Shakespeare, Bill, 142, 143
Shaughnessy, Clark, 146, 147, 148, 149,
    150, 151, 174
Shaver, Gus, 131
Sherman, Rod, 186
Shevlin, Tom, 70
Shrove Tuesday, 5, 11
Simpson, O. J., 186, 195, 196, 197, 198
Sinkwich, Frankie, 155
Slater, Duke, 146
Sloan, Steve, 189
Smith, Charles (Bubba), 187, 191
Snavely, Carl, 144
Snow, Jack, 185
Soccer, 3, 10, 16, 17, 25, 26, 28, 31, 32-
    34, 36, 37, 41, 64, 74
Soldier Field, 120
South, University of, see Sewanee
Southeastern Conference, 172
Southern California, University of, 73,
    129, 130, 131, 132, 148, 159, 172,
    185, 186, 192, 195, 197, 200, 201
Southern Methodist University, 127, 130,
    140, 141, 160, 161, 181, 193, 194
Southwest Conference, 137, 140, 160,
    181, 194
Spears, Clarence W. (Doc), 122, 123,
    124
Speyrer, Cotton, 202
Stabler, Kenny, 177, 195
Stagg, Amos Alonzo, 57, 79, 81-85, 86,
    88, 91, 94, 98, 101, 146, 150, 163,
    190
Stallings, Gene, 194, 195
Standlee, Norm, 148, 149
Stanford University, 75, 85, 87, 88, 91,
    118, 119, 132, 137, 138, 139, 146,
    147, 148, 149, 150, 151, 159, 167,
    172, 200
Staubach, Roger, 181, 182, 183
Steckle, W., 81
Steinmark, Fred, 202
Stephenson, Bob, 196
Stevens, Mal, 126
Stockton College, 83
Street, James (Slick), 201
Strong, Ken, 111, 121
Strupper, Everett, 78
Stubbes, Philip, 6
Sugar Bowl, 164, 176, 212
Susquehanna University, 83
Suter, Herman, 75, 77
Southerland, Dr. John B. (Jock), 129
Swarthmore College, 91
Swiacki, Bill, 151
Swink, Jim, 174
Syracuse University, 104, 106, 132, 169,
    172, 175, 192

T-formation, 46, 147, 148, 149, 150, 151, 165, 168, 171, 174, 200
Tatum, Jim, 151, 164, 165
Tennessee, University of, 76, 129, 174, 192, 195
Terry, Wyllys, 56
Texas, University of, 75, 76, 174, 175, 181, 182, 183, 194, 200, 201, 202
Texas A. & M. University, 76, 127, 144, 176, 177, 178, 193, 194
Texas Christian University, 140, 141, 161, 174
Theismann, Joe, 201, 202
Thomas, Frank, 138
Thompson, Oliver D., 39
Thorpe, Jim, 70, 106-08, 109, 122, 124
Touchdown, Introduction of, 9, 29, 32, 33, 41
Tournament of Roses Association, 87-88
Trafford, Bernie, 62
Trippi, Charley, 155
Tubbs, Jerry, 165
Tucker, Arnold, 156, 159
Tulane University, 76, 133, 150

Uniform, Introduction of, 19, 52
United Press Poll, 171, 189
United States Military Academy, 64, 73, 92, 97, 98-99, 100, 104, 108, 111, 117, 118, 120, 126, 130, 147, 151, 154, 156, 157, 158, 159, 163, 192, 200
United States Naval Academy, 64, 73, 77, 94, 97, 98, 104, 120, 126, 130, 137, 141, 154, 156, 163, 174, 181, 182, 183, 193, 200

Vanderbilt University, 78, 171
Varney, Pete, 199
Veeder, Paul, 97
Vessel, Billy, 165

Wade, Wallace, 138, 154
Walker, Doak, 160, 161

Walsh, Adam, 117, 118
Warmack, Bob, 195
Warner, Glenn (Pop), 70, 94, 97, 104-06, 107-08
Washburn University, 95
Washington, Kenny, 146
Washington, University of, 73, 166, 172
Washington and Jefferson College, 132
Washington Redskins, 140, 141
Watkinson, George, 55
Weatherall, Jim, 165
Webster, George, 191
Weinstock, Izzy, 135
Wesleyan University, 55-56
West Virginia University, 122, 174
Western Conference, 78
White, Byron, 145
Whiting, William A., 31
Whitney, Caspar, 49, 79, 81
Wichita, University of, 95
Wilkinson, Charles (Bud), 135, 151, 164, 165, 174, 175, 178
Williams, H. L., 84, 86
Wilson, Bobby, 140, 141
Wisconsin, University of, 78-79, 80, 81, 118, 123, 141
Wistert brothers, 160
Wojciechowicz, Alex, 141
Woodruff, George W., 63
Worster, Steve, 201

Yale Bowl, 49, 90
Yale University, 12, 13-14, 16, 25, 26-28, 31-34, 35, 37-42, 43, 44, 46-49, 50, 51, 52, 54-57, 61-63, 64, 65, 67, 68, 69-73, 74-75, 78, 79, 83, 91, 94, 97, 100, 103, 110, 121, 126, 136, 137, 172, 195, 198, 199, 200, 204
Yoder, Jim, 201
Yost, Fielding H. (Hurry Up), 85-87, 88, 89-90, 112, 114, 120, 159
Young, Scrapiron, 130

Zimmerman, Kurt, 189
Zuppke, Bob, 111, 112, 114, 115, 116